AIR POWER UAVs: The Wider Context

CONTENTS

UNMANNED AIR VEHICLES : THE WIDER CONTEXT

Foreword by Air Chief Marshal Sir Glenn Torpy

The huge growth in the variety of Unmanned Air Vehicles (UAVs) and their increasing importance in the contemporary operating environment represent one of the most significant and dramatic advances in air power capability over the past decade. Whilst the hard-edged technology of UAVs has been considered in great depth in many publications, conferences and seminars, the 'softer' issues, which in many ways are equally problematic, have been much less widely debated; the surprising richness of the historical record of UAV use is also little known. Consequently, I challenged the assembled academic experts at this Chief of the Air Staff's Workshop to explore these areas in more detail, to develop our understanding of UAVs within a much broader context.

Historically, the development of UAVs has been marked by sporadic periods of very rapid technological advances, usually to provide solutions to particular problems during specific conflicts, punctuated by long spells of stagnation and a return to a reliance on manned aircraft between wars. This process has been cyclical, and the wheel often needed to be reinvented, as previous experience was forgotten or disregarded. While this may have been acceptable in an age of cheap, expendable and relatively low-capability platforms, this is no longer always the case; current UAVs may still be small and virtually disposable, but can also be large, highly complex and capable, with a commensurate price-tag. As airmen, we therefore need to take a much longer-term view of UAV procurement and employment, and accept that they will remain a permanent feature in the order of battle of any capable, modern air force.

UAVs have forced us to rethink some of the basic tenets of air power. Traditionally, the 'impermanence' of air platforms has been a real limitation and while UAVs do not yet have the capability to stay aloft indefinitely, this capability may be on the horizon. Even with current platforms, 'virtual permanence' over significant areas of the battlespace is possible, given the right planning. The legal and ethical perspectives and constraints associated with UAVs must also be fully understood, if their employment is not to be unduly constrained. One critical aspect is the cultural context, not just of the air forces employing the capability, but also within those we are seeking to influence. The psychological impact of remote warfare fought by remote war-fighters is very different from the more traditional uses of military force and the effect on the operators, the enemy, and the people amongst whom we fight, must all be assessed carefully, so that threats can be countered and opportunities taken. If we accept the premise that UAVs are now an integral component of air power delivery, we must be agile in our thinking to understand how we can adapt our organisations, structures, training and recruitment to exploit the military possibilities they offer fully.

The output from the Workshop, captured in this publication, may not contain all the answers, but it does at least expose the questions and highlight issues and challenges for further analysis. This, I believe, provides a useful basis for a more informed and holistic debate about how air forces can best harness the capability offered by UAVs now, and in the future.

Air Chief Marshal Sir Glenn Torpy

INTRODUCTION

Air Cdre Neville Parton

The role of the Chief of the Air Staff's Workshops has remained remarkably constant since first established in the 1980s: to bring together a mix of academics and practitioners in order to shed fresh light on contemporary air power issues. The 2007 workshop was no different, although for the first time the subject matter was related to a particular technological field – that of unmanned air vehicles (UAVs) – rather than the historical or doctrinal subjects that had predominated in the past. It did see the assembling of a unique group of individuals; comprising historians, lawyers, engineers, academics and operators, who spent a considerable period of time discussing both historical and contemporary perspectives on UAV operations, before agreeing on the contents that would make up the breadth and depth of this publication.

The history of UAVs is, perhaps surprisingly, almost as long as the history of flight itself, as the first flying bomb type device was developed during the First World War. Almost every decade during the intervening ninety years has seen advances in this field, although the last ten years in particular has certainly seen an explosion in not only the numbers but also the capability of such platforms. Given such an ancestry, one could be forgiven for wondering whether there were any aspects of UAV operations that have not already been explored over the course of such a lengthy period of operations. However, as the capabilities of UAVs have undergone radical changes in the last decade, driven by advances in technology, the focus has been very much on solving the technical problems associated with their use. There has been an emphasis on control and communication – especially with regard to the large amounts of data that can be produced by the multi-spectral imaging systems common to many modern systems, and other prominent areas for consideration have included decision support and information distribution. Furthermore, given the tremendous lineage of UAV-type platforms, it is interesting to note how frequently lessons in general have had to be re-learnt as development in this field has tendedto run in cycles. In one of the very few publications to look specifically at the history of UAV development, it is noted that: "Over the past 85 years, robotic aircraft have been repeatedly called by the demands of war onto the stage of history to perform and perhaps to advance a step further in technology; then fade back into obscurity at war's end only to rise, phoenix-like, when the next conflict arises. With each reincarnation, lessons learned, some trivial and some significant, are lost in the ashes."[1] Of course problems with learning from experience are nothing new, and hence the inclusion ofa historical element to address just this aspect. Yet there is also a surprising lack of material available on the implications for non-technical areas of the advances that have been made. Topics such as the legal, moral, ethical and cultural aspects have been by and large ignored; yet these have the potential to impact on the utility of UAVs just as much as the more technical elements, and again this gap provides part of the rationale for this publication.

Indeed an observer at recent conferences on UAVs would perhaps have been forgiven for thinking that these were simply seen as an extension of current weapons systems, which would have no impact on the nature of conflict itself beyond reducing the manpower losses of friendly forces and increasing the range and endurance of reconnaissance systems in particular. However the introduction of a class of weapon which allows engagement with the enemy without personal risk surely has to be considered in more than simply technical terms. The introduction of the tank in the First World War saw British tank crews who surrendered after their vehicles were disabled either killed or beaten up by Germans, who had been terrorised by the vehicles and clearly felt that they offered an unfair advantage.[2] A frequently cited Islamist view is that the Western approach to warfare, as exemplified in both Iraq and Afghanistan, is that it depends upon a cowardly way of warfare (air power) which is frequently indiscriminate, killing women and children. Such an approach is then used to justify the outrages practised by such groups as Al Qaeda.[3] Some consideration therefore has to be given to the likely impact of UAVs on war itself.

Some food for thought can be found in the writings of Professor Coker, Professor of International Relations at the London School of Economics and Social Science, who has produced in recent years some remarkable books dealing with likely changes to the nature of warfare itself in the 21st Century.[4] These deal with not only the technological changes that may occur, but also the way in which those changes may alter the very nature of warfare, and in particular warfare between the 'modern' (or even post-modern) world and those who would seek to challenge it. Some of his material comes from the realm of fiction – but fiction that has very rapidly been overtaken by reality. For instance he refers to a short story which centres around soldiers who fight, completely disengaged from the battlefield, in laser-shooting capsules orbiting the Earth. In this construct the rewards of achieving command include the luxury of being able to wear bedroom slippers and take 'personal preference kits' into the capsule.[5] Whilst this might have seemed far distant in 1983, when the piece was written, we are arguably in that world now, where UAVs such as the General Atomic's Reaper and Predator fly in operations over Iraq and Afghanistan, but are controlled from an operating base just outside Las Vegas, Nevada. The reason for Coker's focussing on this particular example is to illustrate the sense of dissociation that such warriors will feel, if the term warrior can justifiably be used for such individuals, and to consider the effect on both them and the conflict in which they are engaged. But the impact is likely to be felt more broadly within a fighting service than just the individuals concerned; there is also the probability of changes in the way that this group of individuals will be perceived by others. Will the UAV operators be perceived as heroic by the troops they support on the ground, or dissociated technicians with no real understanding of the nature of warfare? And what impact will that have in turn on their ability to influence tactics, operational art and strategy?

Moreover effects will also be produced in the wider world. The importance of propaganda in modern conflict was arguably reinforced by the 2006 conflict in the Lebanon between the Israeli Defence Forces (IDF) and Hezbollah – a conflict in which, it is worth noting, the number of UAV flying hours certainly approached if not exceeded those of fixed wing fast-jet aircraft.[6] Here, whilst Israel undoubtedly enjoyed a tremendous level of supremacy in terms of military technology, it seemed unable to translate this into a strategic advantage, especially in the broader political sphere. This certainly seemed to be borne out by the Economist's summary of the campaign, whose banner headline in the week 19th August 2006 proclaimed 'Nasrallah wins the war'. And as William Arkin points out, "Some even argue that Israel's problem is one of perceptions: that the 2006 war was itself a war of competing narratives and Israel failed to "win" the public relations battle…".[7] In his recent publication on the role of propaganda in politics, Nicholas O'Shaughnessy points to the particular effectiveness of negative propaganda in the modern world, as well as the elements that go to make up propaganda – rhetoric, myth and symbolism.[8] In such a construct the use of air power against a sub-state actor is always open to portrayal in David versus Goliath terms, but how much more so if one side is not seen as even being willing to risk the lives of its servicemen in the conflict.[9] Given such a range of issues, the need for a debate in this subject area seems compelling.

Against such a backdrop the aims of this publication are modest – to provide an introduction to some of the issues that armed forces in general, and air forces in particular, will have to come to terms with as UAV usage becomes far more widespread. In terms of content we begin with two historical overviews, which examine the ways in which UAVs have developed, initially from the 1920s up until the introduction of the first reconnaissance vehicles in the 1950s, and then from the 1950s to the present day. Whilst accepting that this represents an arbitrary divide, it does allow for a focus on the very different ways in which the role of the UAV was perceived – something which will be returned to later on. This is followed by an examination of likely developments over the next 40 years, and taken together with the two previous chapters, provides the requisite context within which the subsequent elements are situated. The first of these provides consideration of some of the legal factors that will have to be considered, particularly if greater degrees of autonomy are sought, as well as the potential problems caused by the use of civilian operators for such systems. This is followed by an overview of some of the ethical aspects inherent in the use of UAVs, especially if used in offensive roles, where there are potential implications for the nature of warfare itself, especially in a counter-insurgency environment. However there are also cultural aspects that need to be considered in terms of implications for the user community – or in other words what the implications are for an air force of much greater use of UAVs with regard to its traditional organisation and values. This is explored in some detail, before bringing together the various threads in order to draw not only some conclusions regarding future developments and their implications, but also to make some recommendations about potentially fruitful areas for further study. This latter aspect is particularly important as the workshop was intended to act as an initiator for further work and discussion in the academic arena, rather than being the last word on the subject.

At this point it is also worth recognising that the language used to describe UAVs has gone, and is still undergoing, considerable change. Whilst there is no commonly agreed lexicon, apart from those within individual armed services, there are a number of generic terms that are used, the derivation of some of which are move obvious than others. In order to assist understanding throughout the rest of this publication a very brief etymology is provided at the end of the chapter, in strictly alphabetical order, and with (where possible) an explanation of whence the term was derived. It should be noted that a number of the terms associated with UAV history do not, strictly speaking, refer to what would now be understood as UAVs – a point which is worth addressing.

There is no generally agreed definition of what exactly constitutes a UAV. However, there are a number of characteristics which can be considered in terms of helping to bring the field down to a manageable size. The first two of these are, quite obviously, that the vehicle should be without a human occupant and reliant on aerodynamic lift or buoyancy to remain airborne. Although from a historical perspective a number of one-way UAVs have been considered in this publication, as these provide a greater degree of understanding of how the technologies in particular have evolved, reuseability is also a factor, as this generally removes such entities as missiles and loitering munitions. Size in purely physical terms is probably not a good differentiator, as ever increasing miniaturization means that smaller UAVs can now undertake roles that would have been inconceivable only a few years ago. The US military, and others, have attempted to differentiate in terms of performance, looking at operational ceilings and endurance, resulting in the introduction of tier. However at present no attempt appears to have been made to differentiate in terms of the degree of autonomy that a UAV possesses, or of the overall system requirements needed to operate it. For instance vehicles such as the Predator require a considerable degree of operator skill to actually 'fly', particularly during the landing phase, albeit remotely, whereas a platform such as Global Hawk operates entirely via keyboard and mouse actuated commands: no joystick required. Another set of characteristics that could be used to define UAVs would be to identify them by their role: reconnaissance, surveillance, weapon delivery, supply delivery, communications relay, air defence and so on.

Irrespective of the precise terminology employed, or of the roles for which they may be used, it is clear that technological advances are likely to result in a significant increase in the usage of UAVs by the armed forces. Whilst some of the areas of employment will be uncontroversial, others have the potential to impact significantly both the nature of war and the nature of the armed forces. These changes will not happen immediately, but given the likely trajectory of progress in this area, the need to address the broader aspects of UAV operations is surely now beyond dispute. As ever, the Royal Air Force is keen to stimulate public debate in areas where controversy may arise, and where the need for a debate to identify and clarify the issues is recognised. The aim of this publication is to stimulate and inform the debate: replies will be welcomed via the pages of *Air Power Review*, the RAF's professional air power journal.[10]

NOTES

[1] Laurence R. Newcome, *Unmanned Aviation : A Brief History of Unmanned Aerial Vehicles* (Barnsley: Pen & Sword Aviation, 2004), v.

[2] Richard Holmes, *Acts of War : The Behaviour of Men in Battle* (London: Cassell Military Paperbacks, 2004), 387.

[3] "They also depend on massive air strikes so as to conceal their most prominent point of weakness, which is the fear, cowardliness, and the absence of combat spirit among US soldiers … We stress the importance of the martyrdom operations against the enemy - operations that inflicted harm on the United States and Israel that have been unprecedented in their history, thanks to Almighty God. " BBC News, "Bin Laden Tape: Text," **http://news.bbc.co.uk/1/hi/world/middle_ east/2751019.stm**.

[4] Christopher Coker, *Waging War without Warriors? The Changing Culture of Military Conflict.* (Boulder: Lynne Rieb Publishers, Inc., 2002), 130., ———, *The Future of War : The Re-Enchantment of War in the Twenty-First Century* (Malden: Blackwell Publishing, 2004).

[5] Don DeLillo, "Human Moments in World War Iii," *Esquire*, July 1983.

[6] Gp Capt Neville Parton, "Israel's 2006 Campaign in the Lebanon," *Air Power Review 10*, no. 2 (2007).. It is also worthy of note that this conflict also saw the use of UAVs by both sides, with Hezbollah operating UAVs over Northern Israel.

[7] William M. Arkin, *Divining Victory : Airpower in the 2006 Israel-Hezbollah War* (Alabama: Air University Press, 2007), 150.

[8] Nicholas Jackson O'Shaughnessy, *Politics and Propaganda : Weapons of Mass Seduction* (Ann Arbor: The University of Michigan Press, 2004), 65.

[9] "The computer chip may very well be a most useful war fighting tool. For example, while it is never a good thing when we lose a Predator on the battlefield, given the alternatives I look forward to many more computer chips dying for our country." US Secretary of the Air Force, as quoted in Coker, *The Future of War : The Re-Enchantment of War in the Twenty-First Century*, 130.

[10] **http://www.airpowerstudies.co.uk/airpowerreview.htm**

GLOSSARY

Aerial Torpedo One of the earliest terms used, referring to a non-reusable cruise missile-type platform, specifically designed to deliver a warhead to a target. Derivation was obviously from a parallel with naval torpedoes.

Aerial Target Another early term, for a reusable (albeit generally with a limited life expectancy) target platform – mostly remotely controlled in nature.

Automatically Piloted Vehicle A term which saw some usage predominantly in the 1950s and 1960s, generally used to refer to reconnaissance-type UAVs.

Cruise Missiles A non-reusable platform specifically designed to deliver a warhead to a target. The term was used to make clear that this was very different to a ballistic missile, in that it depended upon aerodynamic lift in order to operate.

Drones An early term for a platform generally designed to act as a target. A number of origins for the term have been suggested, however the most likely is that as a target they would fly with a fixed engine setting over a fixed course, 'droning' along. The term was later used with a descriptor to identify different types, e.g. target drone, reconnaissance drone and so forth.

Flying Bomb A Second World War term for a cruise missile type vehicle.

Guided Bomb Another term that has occasionally been used for a cruise missile-type vehicle.

Micro Air Vehicle (MAV) A generic term for a small UAV. DARPA defines a MAV as being less than 15 cm in any dimension, but this is not a generally accepted definition.[1]

Medium Altitude Long Endurance (MALE) A generic term for a class of UAV that operates in the surface to 30 000 feet region, and with an endurance of up to 12-15 hours.

High Altitude Long Endurance (HALE) A generic term for a class of UAV that is designed to operate above 30 000 feet, and with an endurance of 24 hours plus.

Pilotless Aircraft A term which saw considerable use in the 1920s and 1930s by the British aviation establishment.[2]

Remotely Operated Aircraft (ROA) This term was introduced by the US Federal Aviation Administration, as their legal remit extended specifically to aircraft, not aerial vehicles.

Remotely Operated Vehicle (ROV) This term has generally been used as a maritime equivalent to the RPV (see below), although it has occasionally been used in other environments.

Remotely Piloted Vehicle (RPV) A term that was used, mainly in North America, to identify a vehicle which required a remote operator (as opposed to a completely autonomous system).

Uninhabited/Unmanned[3] Aerial System (UAS) This term has recently been introduced to recognise that a UAV by itself is not useful; without the associated command and control elements such as ground stations and associated relay mechanisms (satellites) it cannot function. The term UAS (or sometimes *UAVS (UAV System)*) is therefore used to refer to the entire system: the platform, command/communication links and the associated ground (or airborne) control stations.

Uninhabited /Unmanned Aerial Vehicles (UAV) A generic term for an air vehicle which has no human operator on board. This can refer to platforms which require direction from a remote operator, or those that are entirely autonomous, and can be either heavier-than-air or lighter-than-air.[4] No differentiation is made regarding the role for which the UAV is intended, other than the recent introduction of the term UCAV (see below).

Uninhabited /Unmanned Combat Aerial Vehicles (UCAV) A term intended to identify a class of UAVs which had an offensive capability, in terms of being able to both carry and release some form of munition. In future this may well include directed energy weapons.

NOTES

[1] See **http://www.defense-update.com/features/du-2-04/mav-darpa.htm** for more information.

[2] For instance the *Larynx* project (see AIR 5/444 in The National Archives).

[3] The term was originally unmanned, but unmanned has been used more in recent years – allegedly as part of the linguistic de-sexing that has also seen the introduction of terms such as chairperson *vice* chairman. Current UK MoD policy is that the term unmanned be used, and hence that approach is followed throughout this publication.

[4] In US Department of Defence definitions, lighter-than-air platforms are excluded from the UAV class.

THE DEVELOPMENT OF UAVS AND UCAVS: THE EARLY YEARS

Dr Christina J. M. Goulter

The desire to put machinery rather than humans in harm's way has always been a feature of military history. Ideas of using unmanned aerial platforms for the purposes of delivering ordnance probably pre-date Classical times, if we consider how the Chinese conceived of using explosive kites in the battlespace, but became more feasible with the advent of balloons during the 19th century. As the balloon age gave way to fixed wing aviation, the possibility of using unmanned platforms also for reconnaissance was investigated by a number of nations, with the United Kingdom and the USA at the forefront of research. As ever, warfare was the 'mother of invention' and great strides were made in Unmanned Aerial Vehicle (UAV) and Unmanned Combat Aerial Vehicle (UCAV) design and conceptualisation in both the First and Second World Wars. By 1945, Germany had overtaken other nations in unmanned platform technology, and this technological lead was quickly acquired by the Americans at the end of the Second World War, with the transfer of many leading German aeronautical scientists to the US. As the Cold War deepened, the US and NATO became interested in UAVs primarily for reconnaissance, especially after the loss of the U2 spyplane over the USSR in 1960. The need to conduct stealthy reconnaissance and surveillance using the less politically inflammatory unmanned platform was given heightened impetus by the Vietnam War, when the US found it necessary to monitor North and South Vietnam's border areas. It can be argued that Vietnam delineates the beginning of modern UAV and UCAV technology and conceptualisation, because the US developed unmanned platforms for a variety of roles in that conflict, including the multi-role UAV. In the early 1970s, the US lead in UAV development was, for a time, overtaken by Israel, but since the late 1980s, the most significant technological advances and conceptual work have been performed by the US.

Modern UAV and UCAV technology owes its existence to a number of developmental threads, including early work on guided bombs and missiles. So although the generally accepted definition of a UAV or UCAV is that the platform must be recoverable, some discussion of non-recoverable guided systems is required in order to understand current technologies and their employment. What is more difficult to trace is the conceptual work which surrounded some of the early UAV and UCAV technologies. In some cases, the uses to which certain platforms were to be put remains a matter of conjecture. In other cases, very advanced conceptualisation appears not to have outlived a particular UAV or UCAV programme and important lessons were filed away, only to be rediscovered comparatively recently. However, even a brief survey treatment of early UAV and UCAV development provides a useful guide to the strengths and weaknesses of such systems, including the cost-benefits of their employment compared with manned platforms. As a general rule, interest in unmanned systems has been greatest, not surprisingly, when the threat to manned platforms has been serious or when political sensitivities precluded manned surveillance.

Early unmanned aerial vehicle development can be said to divide into two main periods. The first encompasses balloon flight in the 19th Century and attempts to use balloons as unmanned aerial bombers, through to First World War aerial torpedoes which were equipped with basic guidance apparatus.[1] The second period began during the 1930s, with the advent of radio-controlled, recoverable drones. The ability both to control and recover an unmanned platform demarcates this latter group as the true precursors of modern UAVs and UCAVs. However, the first period is interesting because some of the conceptual work was remarkably modern.

One of the earliest records of the use of an unmanned aerial vehicle in the battlespace occurred during the Italian Wars of Unification. In August 1849, the Austrians attacked Venice with unmanned balloons armed with high explosive. The success of these attacks was entirely dependent on favourable winds and a balloon's range was limited by the length of a copper wire, through which a detonating charge would run. Just over a decade later, during the American Civil War, an inventor, Charles Perley, registered a patent for an unmanned 'aerial bomber' which built on the European experience. Perley's design comprised a hot air balloon carrying explosives, which would arm themselves on release from the balloon's basket. A pre-set timing device would dictate when the basket released its load. Both Union and Confederate Armies employed the 'Perley Bomber', with varying degrees of success. On a number of occasions, changes in wind direction caused balloons to drop their loads over friendly forces, and out of this experience came the requirement for some type of guidance system. However, it would be another sixty years before remote control guidance technology became a reality, but it at least demonstrates that the idea of remote control existed well before the First World War.

In the United Kingdom, meanwhile, the possibility of using kites for aerial reconnaissance seemed feasible when, in 1883, the photographer Douglas Archibald used cameras mounted on kites to take low altitude photographs. Archibald's photographs were widely published, and the first military interest in the concept came from the US Army. During the Spanish-American War of 1898, the US Army employed kite cameras to obtain essential intelligence on enemy dispositions and fortifications. This was the first recorded use of the third dimension for intelligence gathering purposes, and it is interesting to note that the US Army's fledgling G2 organisation thereafter considered aerial photography as one of their key sources for ORBAT analysis. Thereafter, technical means of gathering intelligence became a very strong thread in the US intelligence trade.[2]

The First World War heightened interest in remote systems for both reconnaissance and strike purposes, with the greatest effort being expended in the latter area. The USA, Germany and the UK had very similar research and development programmes devoted to 'glide bombs' (forerunners of the German V-1 weapon). The Germans began their research as early as 1915, and by the end of the war, Siemens research laboratories had produced gliders capable of carrying over 2,000 lb loads over ranges of about 5 to 7 miles. Although none of the research resulted in an operational platform before the Armistice, this early work laid the basis of research into the V-1 some twenty years later.[3]

In Britain, the first research into unmanned platforms occurred in 1916. The three biggest aeronautical industries (Sopwith, de Havilland and the Royal Aircraft Factory) all successfully produced unmanned aircraft in 1917, and the greatest successes were achieved by the Royal Aircraft Factory with the testing of three radio controlled aircraft. However, with the end of the war, the RAF's interest in unmanned aircraft fell away abruptly as budget cuts wiped out most research and development.[4]

After the American entry into the war in 1917, the US Navy took the lead in research and development in the field and expressed particular interest in flying bombs. It sponsored development of the so-called Sperry Aerial Torpedo, which was a 300lb bomb mounted on a remotely controlled Curtiss training aircraft. In 1917, this succeeded in flying 50 miles. A similar concept was sponsored by the US Army Air Corps, which resulted in the 'Kettering Bug', a remotely controlled bi-plane, also designed to take a 300lb ordnance load. However, although the US military ordered large numbers of these remotely controlled platforms, the end of the First World War saw a rapid winding down of research and development into 'flying bombs', and interest was not resuscitated until the late 1930s, in part as a result of British experiments into radio-controlled target drones.[5]

In the early 1930s, the Royal Navy issued a requirement for a remote-controlled target drone for gunnery practice. This requirement came out of the infamous 'Bomber versus Battleship' debates over the vulnerability of the UK's capital ships which preoccupied the Admiralty and the Air Staff during the 1920s, early 1930s. The RAF had claimed that the advent of the bomber meant that any nation's capital ships were now under threat, whereas the Royal Navy argued that developments in armour plating, gunnery and ship speeds meant that aerial attack was unlikely to succeed. A series of bombing trials satisfied neither party, so the Royal Navy was intent on proving, beyond any reasonable doubt, that any aircraft coming within range of capital ships equipped with the latest gunfire control systems would not survive. Therefore, the Navy modified a number of Fairey IIIF reconnaissance floatplanes to act as target drones. These 'Fairey Queens', as they were known, were successfully trialled in the Mediterranean during September 1932, and each time they were tested, they survived what was apparently heavy gunfire. This prompted calls for more rigorous experimentation, and led to the development of the first true recoverable and reusable UAV, the so-called

'Queen Bee', which was a radio-controlled development of the de Havilland Tiger Moth trainer. Between 1934 and the end of the Second World War, no fewer than 420 'Queen Bees' were built for the Royal Navy. It is worth noting that 'Queen Bee' experimentation led the Royal Navy to conclude that it could not rely purely on large calibre guns for shipborne defence, and, as a result, the Admiralty called for increased employment of close-range 'pom-pom' guns to supplement the heavy guns. Therefore, it can be said that the 'Queen Bee' contributed to the Navy's concept of layered defence, which remains the cornerstone of modern surface fleet defence.[6]

During the late 1930s, the Americans also developed radio-controlled drones for gunnery practice. A recent British émigré, Reginald Denny, who had served as an Air Gunner in the Royal Flying Corps, formed the Radioplane Company in the mid-1930s. Denny's aim was to provide a low cost aircraft drone which he could provide to both the US Navy and the US Army Air Corps. After lengthy experimentation, Denny won a contract with the US Army Air Corps in 1930 for the RP-4 Radioplane, and by the end of the Second World War, his company had manufactured 15,000 drones for the US Services. It is unclear from the surviving records as to how much cross-fertilisation went on between the British and American drone programmes, but it appears that the RP-4 was an independent invention based on Denny's experiences in the First World War. However, this work laid the foundation for wartime development of radio-controlled aircraft used as flying bombs. Both the US Navy and the US Army Air Forces experimented with unmanned bombers, such as the B-17 and B-24, loaded with 20,000lbs of high explosive for use against high value enemy targets. The USAAF programme, given the code name of *Aphrodite*, involved launching a bomber, manned by a pilot and chief technician, who would set the radio-control device in flight, prime the ordnance, and then bale out while still over the English countryside. The first *Aphrodite* raid occurred on 4 August 1944 against German V-weapon sites in France. Although this had limited impact, because many of the bombers were shot down before they reached their targets or went off course, one of the most interesting proposals to emerge from this programme was the idea of fitting a television monitor in the nose of the *Aphrodite* bomber so that it could be directed onto its target with greater precision.[7]

At the end of the Second World War, American and British aeronautical scientists were surprised to discover the substantial lead which the Germans had in the field of radio-guided missiles. Although the German military was heavily constrained by the terms of the Versailles Treaty after the First World War, the German Army, in particular, maintained its interest in guided bomb research throughout the 1920s. Ironically, the constraints imposed by the Treaty of Versailles, which prevented the Germans from producing large scale conventional forces, compelled research into alternative weapons and alternative materials, including aluminium alloys. In 1931, the Wehrmacht took control over missile research, and co-opted the services of a number of gifted aerospace engineers, including Wehrner von Braun, who had come to the Wehrmacht's attention in 1929 because of his rocket theorems. Not to be outdone, Hermann Goering, head of the Luftwaffe, established a separate rocket research facility, with the specific brief of experimenting with liquid-fuel propulsion systems. The serious rivalry which existed between the Wehrmacht and Luftwaffe high commands meant that these two main research strands were not brought together in a coherent way before the Second World War. Had this happened, then the outcome of the Second World War may have been very different, and this was an important lesson noted by the Americans at the end of the war, because the US Department of Defence was placed in overall control of all military technological development.[8]

One of the most striking features of German missile development is the sheer number of models produced. This can be explained, in large part, by interference from Hitler and the climate of fear he created among his subordinates as he pushed for systems which would provide the Germans with some comparative advantage over the Allies. In addition to the most common V-weapons, the Wehrmacht and Luftwaffe between them sponsored the development of over 200 various guided and gliding bombs, and surface-to-air, air-to-surface and air-to-air missiles. The various projects are too numerous to discuss here, but a number of them demonstrate just how far the German technical lead had become by the end of the Second World War, and, because of the technology transfer to the Western Allies at the end of the war, underpinned American aeronautical research for at least another thirty years. One of the uncomfortable facets of this technology transfer at the end of the war is the fact that most of the German secret weapons research and development was dependent upon slave labour, and this is particularly true of both the V-1 and V-2. Many moral questions were swept under the carpet after 1945 because of the deteriorating East-West relations. Although a full discussion of the moral implications of technology transfer lies beyond the scope of this discussion, it demands some mention. It is also worth noting that this would not be the last time democracies at war faced totalitarian regimes which could, by their very nature, resource spectacular projects without most of the usual constraints.[9]

The German research and development to have had the greatest influence on Western air power is undoubtedly the V-weapons programme, so-called because they were intended as 'vengeance weapons' *(vergeltungswaffe)*. The V-1 is of particular importance to this discussion as it was the first large scale operational employment of unmanned aircraft. Although both the Wehrmacht and the Luftwaffe had been experimenting with unmanned platforms during the late 1930s, the single biggest impetus to develop further a pilotless missile was the German defeat in the Battle of Britain. The German hierarchy wanted to maintain pressure on Britain, while preparing for the offensive in the East, against the Soviet Union. The V-weapon was seen as a simple and relatively cheap means of maintaining the pressure without expending precious trained aircrew and manned, multi-role platforms. Hitler played a decisive role in speeding up V-weapons development. By mid-1943, the Luftwaffe had fallen out of favour with Hitler because of its failure to subdue Britain, campaign reversals in North Africa, Sicily and on the eastern front, and he was now more interested in the winning potential of secret weapons. So, in the summer of 1943, the V-1 programme was given priority.[10]

The V-1 was a relatively basic aircraft design, with a wingspan of just under 20 feet and cigar-shaped fuselage of 26 feet in length. The operational variants had a warhead of 1,000lbs of High Explosive and a range of 200 miles. Guidance of the weapon was provided by a gyroscope governed by a magnetic compass, which was pre-set before launch. Altitude was controlled by a standard aneroid barometer, which kept the V-1 at 1,000 feet en route to its target, and its range was pre-set by an air log device. Once the requisite range had been reached, the engine was cut, forcing the V-1 into a dive. As the weapon flew in free-fall to the target, it had limited velocity, and this meant that the blast effect was maintained largely above ground. This is what made the V-1 a substantial weapon system, especially when it fell into urban areas, where the blast effect tended to be disproportionately large. The V-1 lacked the accuracy to strike targets other than large centres of population, but this fact heightened its terror value.[11]

The original German concept for V-1 was truly awesome. The plan was to bombard Britain as early as mid-December 1943, with three daily waves, with 300 missiles in each wave. Fortunately, attacks by Bomber Command on one of the main V-weapons production sites at Kassel delayed the operational employment of the V-1 until mid-June 1944, but British intelligence had already identified the new weapon threat. In November 1943, imagery analysis and SIGINT intercepts from the main testing facility at Peenemunde, on the Baltic coast, had highlighted V-1 development, and it was concluded that the weapons could be used against Britain within weeks. IMINT and other intelligence had established the rapid building of multiple launch sites along the French coast. Both Bomber Command and the US 8th Air Force were re-tasked to devote some of their effort to attacking these sites. However, initial attacks proved relatively ineffectual, destroying only seven out of the 69 sites identified. Thereafter, the main bombing effort was directed against the road and rail network in northern France, Belgium and eastern Germany with the aim of interdicting the resupply of these sites. In the months and weeks leading up to D-Day, this bombing became part of the wider 'transportation plan' in support of the invasion, so it is difficult to discern how much effort was devoted specifically with the counter- V-1 campaign in mind. But the proportion of effort devoted to the destruction of these sites does become clearer after D-Day, when up to half of Bomber Command and the 8th Air Forces' tonnage was dropped on V-1 launch areas and facilities associated with the emerging V-2 threat. The official historian of the strategic bombing campaign suggests that attacks on these sites during the second half of 1944 'retarded' and 'reduced' the V-weapon campaign against Britain.[12]

Defence against the V-1 closer to home was also very problematic. As the V-1 could travel at speeds up to 400 miles an hour, only the latest mark of Spitfire had a chance of catching the V-1s. Even then, shooting them down was hazardous, as the blast shrapnel often impacted on the attacker. So, a technique of intercepting and flying alongside the V-1, with the object of tipping its wing, was adopted in most cases. However, this was entirely dependent on timely forewarning of a V-1 assault, and as the transit time between launch and southern England was only 22 minutes, on average, this gave the interceptors little time to find and hunt down their prey. This prompted a rapid redeployment of anti-aircraft guns to a concentrated belt on the south coast, leaving the area behind for 'mopping up' by the RAF if V-1s succeeded in getting through the AAA barrage. By mid-July, the defences in combination had succeeded in reducing the daily assault on Britain from 70 down to about 25, but this meant that a sizeable number of V-1s were still getting through, and there was justifiable concern that civilian morale was crumbling in the face of the new threat, coming as it did on top of general war weariness.[13]

Once the initial V-1 assault was confirmed as a success, the Germans engaged in further conceptual work, including the idea of launching V-1s from manned bombers. This was given priority in case they needed to continue an offensive against Britain from bases inside Germany, following an anticipated withdrawal from France and the Low Countries. Between 9 July and the end of December 1944, nearly 1,600 V-1s were air launched from Heinkel III bombers, one-fifth of the total number of V-1s directed against Britain, with the same rates of success as the land-launched variant. Of the total number of V-1s launched against Britain, 1,847 were destroyed by fighter aircraft, 1,878 by AAA, and 232 by barrage balloons. The majority of the remainder fell in open countryside, but the 2,419 which reached metropolitan London caused 6,184 deaths and 17,981 others were seriously injured. The V-1 offensive had also caused widespread damage in the south-east and over 1,000 factories were affected either directly or indirectly as a result of bomb damage. Absenteeism was also reported to be higher than at any other time during the war, with a 10% fall in industrial production being attributed just to the V-weapon offensive.[14]

Not surprisingly, therefore, when the German V-2 rocket attacks began in September 1944, there were elaborate efforts to disguise the true nature of the latest German 'vengeance' weapon, including press releases to pass off V-2 hits as gas explosions. It was felt that the difficulty of defending against V-2 weapon, because of its supersonic speed, would cause widespread alarm. The V-2 development, while lying slightly outside the scope of this discussion, is worth recounting briefly because it proved that the Germans were at least ten years ahead of their nearest rival, the Americans, in both rocket and radio-guidance systems research, and the guidance system developed for the V-2 would later form the basis of post-war American research into unmanned platforms and missiles.

German experimentation in rocket design went back as far as the early 1930s, and even before the outbreak of war, the German High Command issued a requirement for a high velocity weapon which could hit London and Paris. The first test firings of what would ultimately become the V-2 occurred in 1937, but the major constraint on development was its guidance system. Rockets were prone to go off course as soon as they were launched. This was partly a function of the size of the weapon (it stood at over 46 feet tall and was over 5 feet wide) and its payload. But most of the difficulty arose out of having to control combustion and exhaust velocities (the V-2 required a load of 8,300 lbs of fuel and 11,000 lbs of liquid oxygen, being burnt at a rate of 275 lbs per second). So, a complex system of cybernetic controls was developed to keep the rocket stable in its initial launch and flight path. However, unlike the V-1 which was not radio-controlled, the V-2 had to have some type of radio guidance, and this was the first instance of radar beams being used to guide the trajectory and path of a missile system. Had the war extended beyond 1945, the Allies would have developed means to interfere with the radio-guidance of the V-2, as they had already achieved success against the Luftwaffe's navigational beams earlier in the war. In all, a total of 4,320 V-2s were fired between 6 September 1944 and 27 March 1945. Of these, 1,120 were fired at London, and 2,500 at other Allied targets in France and Belgium.[15]

It is often suggested that the V weapons caused a disproportionate amount of fear and effort. However, if we consider that conventional bombing of Britain resulted in 51,509 killed and over 61,000 seriously injured throughout the whole of the war, the impact that these weapons had during a period of less than one year, it can be said that the German hierarchy achieved much of what it sought to achieve, namely, psychological pressure on the British populace.[16]

The V-weapons programmes spawned a number of other technologies worthy of note. As the Allied bomber offensive increased its stranglehold over the Third Reich, the German hierarchy called for a dual track research effort into anti-aircraft missiles. The most advanced anti-aircraft missile to be developed was the *Wasserfall*, which could reach altitudes in excess of 25,000 feet. This was a derivative of the V-2, and was designed to destroy bomber formations. The missile was to be guided to its target by two radar signals, one homing in on the target and the other tracking the missile's progress. A proximity fuse would then denote the missile. Some 35 trial launches were made, but it is unclear from the historical record as to whether *Wasserfall* ever entered operational service and research and development was halted in February 1945. The *Wasserfall* also benefited from other research into guided missiles for use in air-to-surface roles. As early as 1940, the Luftwaffe had submitted an operational requirement for a guided anti-shipping missile, and this led to the development of a series of radio-controlled glide bombs. The first of these, known as the *Fritz* Fx-1400, was successfully employed against the Italian fleet in September 1943 as it prepared to surrender to the Allies, and it is interesting to note that the Allies suffered more ship losses to *Fritz* guided bombs in the Mediterranean than to conventional attacks. To outward appearances, the *Fritz* looked like a standard 3,000 lb bomb, but what differentiated from the standard specification was that it had control surfaces which were radio-guided from a 'parent' aircraft. A similar guided bomb was the Henschel 293, which was based on a 1,000 lb bomb with wings and fins, and an engine suspended underneath. It relied on electrical impulses transmitted by a 'parent' aircraft via wire guidance to direct it onto a target, and one variant transmitted television images of the target to the controller.[17]

The use of television in guided bombs predated the cruise missile guidance system by some fifty years, and was also well in advance of similar American research during the Second World War. In response to mounting losses among bomber aircrews of the US Army Air Forces, especially the 8th and 15th Air Forces, which operated over Europe, a call was made to increase research into glide bombs. Trials in the spring of 1944 were disappointing because guided glide bombs were not achieving anticipated rates of accuracy. In an effort to improve accuracy, a basic TV camera was fitted into what became known as the GB-4 glide bomb. Others were fitted with infra-red and light-seeking devices. However, none of these entered service before the end of the war.[18]

Both the Western Allies and the Soviets were to benefit greatly from German research, and it is unlikely that either would have got into space so quickly had it not been for technology transfer in 1945. In the meantime, in the USA, captured technology was put to good use in a variety of experimental and practical programmes. Remote control technology was utilised in Operation *Crossroads*, when remotely piloted aircraft were used to take air samples during the US atomic bomb tests of 1946-47. However, the most significant use of German jet engine and missile guidance systems was seen in the post-war first generation of cruise missiles and remotely piloted drones. The V-2 underpinned the development of half a dozen early Cold-War cruise missiles, including the *Snark, Navaho, Matador, Mace,* and *Regulus*. There was a requirement for a cruise missile which could deliver a 2,000 lb warhead over a distance of at least 2,000 miles. Most of these were launched from ramps, and had average cruising speeds of 600 miles per hour. In the early 1960s, these and successor systems were fitted with experimental Automatic Terrain and Navigation (ATRAN) systems, forerunners of the guidance systems used in the Tomahawk cruise missile. This meant that the missiles equipped with ATRAN were no longer reliant on radar monitoring or radio guidance. It marked a substantial leap forward in unmanned guidance technology which would not be improved upon until the 1980s with the advent of satellite global positioning systems. Not all of these early cruise missile variants entered service, and, by the late 1950s, this line of development was overtaken by what was considered to be a more promising method of delivering conventional and nuclear weapons, the ICBM.[19]

However, the German legacy lived on in another strand of US unmanned research: the drone. In the early 1950s, there was a tri-Service requirement for target drones for air-to-air and surface-to-air gunnery and missile training. Out of this requirement emerged the Teledyne Ryan Q-2 *Firebee*. Powered by a turbo-jet engine, the *Firebee* had a wingspan of 12 feet, length of 22 feet, maximum speed of 600 knots and a range of just under 700 miles. Like the latest modern UAV platforms, the greatest advantage of the *Firebee* was found to be its adaptability. It was used first as a gunnery training drone, but was then trialled as a reconnaissance platform and a potential UCAV, and also like the latest generation of unmanned platforms, it was recoverable. Therefore, it can be said that the *Firebee* represents the beginning of modern unmanned technology and conceptualisation.[20]

Research into drones for operational purposes began during the late 1950s, when the US recognised the requirement for an unmanned platform which could perform high altitude reconnaissance. This requirement was given added impetus in May 1960 when the US lost its first U-2 spy plane over the Soviet Union, and the Soviets gained considerable political capital out of the capture of its pilot, Gary Powers. A few months later, an ELINT aircraft was lost over the Barents Sea, killing all on board. The pressure was now on to find a platform which could perform a number of intelligence collection roles. The reconnaissance requirement called for a platform which had a range of some 1,500 miles, a cruising altitude of 55,000 feet, and the ability to take high resolution photographs from this altitude. It was also suggested that the UAV should have a low radar signature, using radar absorbing paint and a means of disguising the air intakes. The latest Teledyne Ryan *Firebee* variant (the Q2-C) won the contract, and this was put through extensive testing during 1962.[21]

The Cuban Missile Crisis in 1962 graphically demonstrated the need for timely intelligence gathering, while at the same time highlighting the political sensitivities attached to manned overflight. On 14 October of that year, a US reconnaissance aircraft detected the installation of Soviet missiles in Cuba, and daily U-2 reconnaissance of Cuba continued until two weeks later, when one of these aircraft was shot down by a SAM missile. As a consequence, the UAV procurement programme was quickly given top priority. Over the next two months, modified *Firebees* performed both photographic reconnaissance and ELINT missions over Cuba, and such was the success of these operations, the *Firebee* was then employed officially by the USAF's 4080th Strategic Reconnaissance Wing. What followed was the most extensive use of UAVs for reconnaissance purposes ever seen in air power history.[22]

Within four days of the Gulf of Tonkin incident, which prompted official US military involvement in Vietnam, the 4080th Strategic Reconnaissance Wing deployed to Okinawa to begin *Firebee* reconnaissance missions over North Vietnam and southern China. The aim of the reconnaissance was to monitor the amount of war materiel being supplied by China to North Vietnam and also to assess the scale of cross-border sanctuaries being used by the North Vietnamese Army for training purposes. During September 1964, several reconnaissance missions were undertaken by UAVs, launched from parent C-130 aircraft, also based on Okinawa. The *Firebees* were then recovered on Taiwan. As the UAV had no landing gear, it deployed a parachute on completion of its mission, and was repatriated back to Okinawa. From the end of 1964, these reconnaissance missions were flown from bases in theatre, with the main base near Saigon, Bien Hoa, acting as the principal focus of reconnaissance capability. Typical reconnaissance missions flew north out of Bien Hoa, flew over the large naval and USMC air base at Da Nang, which allowed the ground controller at Da Nang to check the parent aircraft's course, and release of the UAV usually occurred between Da Nang and the Demilitarised Zone. The *Firebee's* progress was then monitored by the Airborne Remote Control Officer aboard the parent aircraft (usually a C-130).[23]

These early UAV missions suffered a number of losses. The first loss occurred over China on 15 November 1964, and by the following April, four others had been claimed by Chinese ground based defences. Although the origin of the UAVs was obvious, and *Firebee* wreckage was put on display in Beijing, the US government made no comment and the Chinese made very little political capital out of these losses. This had proved the theory that unmanned platforms would be less politically inflammatory than manned aircraft should they be shot down. Meanwhile, manned reconnaissance, mainly by U-2s, continued over North Vietnam until 1965, at which point the North Vietnamese acquired SAMs from the Soviets. Therefore, the requirement for unmanned reconnaissance grew exponentially from this point.[24]

The year of 1965 also coincided with the beginning of the large scale coercive bombing campaign against North Vietnam, Operation *Rolling Thunder*, and the need for targeting intelligence and Battle Damage Assessment reconnaissance had to be given top priority. As the campaign developed, the North Vietnamese posed an increasing number of challenges to US Air Superiority. Not only did the number of SAMs fired increase from around 400 in 1965 to and annual rate of nearly 7,000 three years later, but the number of AAA sites also increased exponentially. Then, in 1966, the US Air Force and US Navy aircrews operating over North Vietnam noticed a mounting air-to-air threat posed by MiG-21s. In the face of these multiple hazards, *Firebee* drones were modified in order to meet a variety of reconnaissance roles. One variant was fitted with a Low Altitude Barometric Control System, which allowed it to fly at ultra-low levels to avoid North Vietnamese radar. Another variant was modified to fly at very high altitude, and another, known as the 147E, was designed to meet the requirement for an ELINT platform. This particular model proved invaluable for assessing the nature of the SAM's guidance system and its fusing mechanism, and this intelligence was used subsequently by SAM suppression aircraft (Wild Weasels) and was, therefore, credited with saving scores of American aircrew and aircraft. The *Firebee* went on to save yet more lives in another capacity. Target drones were employed in what would be recognised today as a 'strike package' concept, whereby they flew below manned strike aircraft and high altitude reconnaissance drones, drawing enemy fire. Later in the war, *Firebee* target drones were used to draw fire away from B-52s operating over North Vietnam. Following successes with CHAFF dispensing drones in 1967-68, additional experimentation also proved the worth of the *Firebee* as an Electronic Counter-Measures platform.[25]

By the middle of the Vietnam War, therefore, the drone had already proved itself as an extremely flexible and capable multi-role platform. In 1969, the loss of a manned ECM aircraft, an EC-121 Super Constellation, with 31 personnel on board, spurred the development of a drone capable of data collection and transmission. This model, known as the 147TE, could collect electronic intelligence from a range of 600 miles from its parent aircraft. This marked a true revolution in ECM technology, because a drone fitted with ten receivers could collect the same amount of data as a manned ECM platform, such as the EC-121, and relay the data instantaneously.[26]

By the end of the Vietnam War, great strides had also been made in photographic reconnaissance. The *Firebee* photographic reconnaissance models available in 1967-68 had operational ceilings of up to 66,000 feet and a range of over 400 miles, and could photograph a 22 mile wide strip along a pre-determined track of 800 miles. By 1972, the 147SC model was fitted with an all round horizon perspective, and the onboard cameras were capable of continuous photographic coverage along a 155 mile path, with resolutions of less than one-third of a metre. Course corrections in this model were also achieved by Doppler radar. The 147SC model performed 1,651 operational missions in the last two years of the Vietnam War, and a late war modification also saw the 147SC *Firebee* used in night reconnaissance, and some drones were equipped with infra-red sensors.[27]

Throughout the whole of the Vietnam War, drones (mainly *Firebees*) performed 3,435 sorties in their various roles. The biggest advocates of UAV employment, perhaps not surprisingly, became the fighter and reconnaissance aircrews, who did not want to repeat their Vietnam experience when drones had more than proved that they could do the job. Had the American involvement in Vietnam gone on for another year, it is probable that *Firebees* would have been employed as unmanned bombers. Experimentation into cruise missiles had been going on since the autumn of 1971, when the US Navy fired a number of *Firebee* Low Altitude Ship to Ship Homing Missiles (FLASH) in an attempt to match the latest Soviet anti-shipping missile, the *Styx*. The FLASH was designed to fly at an altitude of 300 feet, descending to 25 feet in order to deliver a payload of two 500lb bombs. In other experiments, *Firebees* were modified to carry *Maverick* missiles for potential use against SAM sites. However, the American decision in 1968 to withdraw from Vietnam meant that most of this experimentation was not fully funded by the US Defence Department, and it was left to another nation, Israel, to pick up the reins of UCAV development.[28]

During the 1970s, Israel secretly purchased twelve *Firebees* from the USA, and modified them to their own specification, known as *Firebee* 1241s. These played important roles in the 1973 Yom Kippur war between Israel, Egypt and Syria, acting as surveillance platform, decoy drones and also UCAVs. On the second day of the war, the Israeli Air Force used *Firebees* to lead attacks on Egyptian air defences along the Suez Canal. The Egyptians fired most of their SAMs at this first wave of UCAVs, and the *Firebees* successfully evaded 32 of the SAMs, and destroyed 11 others with *Shrike* anti-radar missiles. This success was noted by the Americans, but, remarkably, the US did not reinvigorate research into Uavs and UCAVs until the late 1980s.[29]

It was during the decade after the Vietnam and Yom Kippur Wars that the Israelis took the lead in UAV and UCAV research and development. They quickly became world leaders in small UAV technology for surveillance of the battlespace and urban environment, in particular. In 1978, Israel Aircraft Industries led the way with the *Scout*, a piston-engined UAV with a wingspan of 13 feet, made from fibreglass. The Israelis had been conducting experiments with low-radar signature aircraft, and fibreglass was assessed as the ideal material for a small platform of this type. The *Scout* could transmit real time, 360 degree surveillance via a television camera mounted in the central turret of the UAV. Its greatest operational success occurred during the 1982 Bekaa Valley conflict between Israel, Lebanon and Syria. Israel used a fleet of *Scouts* to search for Syrian SAM missile sites, and having located all but two of these sites, the Israeli Air Force was able to destroy them and gain the initiative. The Israelis went on to inflict serious damage on the Syrian Air Force, as they lost 86 aircraft, for the loss of just one Israeli aircraft, and this Air Superiority advantage allowed the Israelis full freedom of manoeuvre. Therefore, it can be said that the *Scouts* played an essential part in preparation of the battlespace. A further development of the *Scout* was called the *Pioneer*, and this could accommodate ECM equipment as well as surveillance cameras. Like the *Scout*, this was guided either by a predetermined programme linked to an autopilot or by a ground controller. During the late 1980s, the US purchased 20 *Pioneers*, and these were utilised extensively by the US Army during Gulf War I and remain in use within the US military.[30]

The first Gulf War of 1991 delineates the beginning of modern UAV and UCAV technology and conceptualisation. The preceding discussion demonstrates that modern platforms and their integration into the current battlespace owes much to multiple technological and conceptual threads, some of which date as far back as the 19th Century. A broad survey of unmanned development highlights a number of important issues. First, the acceptance of Uavs and UCAVs as proper constituents of force structure is much earlier than most people would suppose.[31] Second, the idea that unmanned platforms can and should be substitutes for manned systems has been surprisingly common among aircrews. However, thirdly, interest in and government funding for unmanned platforms has been episodic in most countries, driven mainly by operational requirements. The US experience is a good case in point. The US military became very interested in Uavs and UCAVs out of necessity during the Second World War and then again during Vietnam, but then lost interest in the decade following Vietnam. Given the heightened sensitivity to casualties brought about by the Vietnam War, and the fact that the main US military operations during the late 1970s, early 1980s tended to be covert (especially in South America), this is an interesting finding. Fourth, and related to the above point, is the fact that nations which became leading advocates or operators of unmanned technology have been heavily dependent on the research and development performed by other nations in order either to kick-start or reinvigorate their own UAV and UCAV programmes. Most of today's leading unmanned platform producers do not have uninterrupted programmes as part of their heritage. When one considers the great advances which were made during some conflicts, such as the Vietnam War in areas such as ECM and high resolution photographic reconnaissance capabilities, this uneven investment has had serious implications. Finally, in spite of this episodic and uneven historical development, it is still possible to argue that unmanned platforms have played substantial and often decisive roles in a number of conflicts. During the Second World War, the German V-weapons programme, in particular, had the potential to seriously weaken British morale and certainly caused a major diversion of air power and intelligence resources in an effort to counter the threat. During conflicts such as the Vietnam War, unmanned platforms proved to be far less politically inflammatory than manned platforms for surveillance and reconnaissance purposes, and their worth as weapons platforms for preparation of the battlespace was amply demonstrated by the Israelis in 1982 in the Bekaa Valley. In all of these cases, the UAVs and UCAVs saved lives, which is the ultimate litmus test for the nations employing them.

NOTES

[1] On board gyroscopic guidance.

[2] **www.pbs.org-NOVA**

[3] Armitage, M. *Unmanned Aircraft* (Brassey's, London, 1988), p. 1.

[4] *Ibid.*

[5] *Ibid*, pp.2-3.

[6] National Archives, AIR 19/138. Bombing trials with HMS *Centurion*, 1929: Summary of Results; Covering note by Air Staff, dd. 1 Nov 1929; Report entitled: 'Bombing trials against HMS *Centurion*' by Air Marshal E. L. Ellington, 14 Oct 1929; AIR 9/4. Air Staff memo: 'The present position with regard to the Air versus Guns controversy', dd. Sept 1930. See also ADM 1/8613. Reports on bombing attacks against HMS *Agamemnon*, 1921; AIR 8/85. Summary of Great Britain's bombing trials carried out in 1921, 1922, 1923 and 1924; Goulter, CJM. *A Forgotten Offensive: Royal Air Force Coastal Command's Anti-Shipping Campaign*, 1940-1945 (Frank Cass, 1995), Chaps 2-3.

[7] Gatland, K. *Development of the Guided Missile* (London, Iliffe, 1952), Chap.5; Armitage, *op. cit.*, pp. 30-33.

[8] Parson, N. *Guided Missiles in War and Peace* (Harvard University Press, Cambridge, 1956), p.21; Ford, B. *German Secret Weapons: Blueprint for Mars* (Ballantine, 1969), p.55.

[9] For a discussion of technology transfer at the end of the Second World War, see Uttley, MRH. 'Operation Surgeon' and Britain's Post-War Exploitation of Nazi German Aeronautics', *Intelligence and National Security*, Vol.17, No.2, Summer 2002, pp.1-26.

[10] Armitage, *op. cit.*, pp.7-10.

[11] *Ibid.*, pp.8-9.

[12] Webster, C. and Frankland, N. *The Strategic Air Offensive Against Germany*, Vol. III (HMSO, 1961), p.296. See also pp. 36, 39, 41-48; Hinsley, H. et al. *British*

Intelligence in the Second World War, Vol. III, Part 2 (HMSO, 1988), pp.536-545; Armitage, op. cit., pp.10-13.

[13] Hinsley, *op. cit.* pp.533-535, 622.

[14] Armitage, *op. cit.*, p.16.

[15] Gatland, *op. cit.*, p. 137. See also Chaps 5-6.

[16] *Ibid*.

[17] Gatland, K. *op. cit.*, Chap.5; Armitage, *op. cit.*, pp.24-28, 30-33. For the technical details of these systems, see **www.ctie.monash.edu/hargrave/ rpav**

[18] Armitage, pp.25-27.

[19] *Ibid.*, Chap 5.

[20] *Ibid.*, p.65.

[21] *Ibid.*, p.65; Jones, C. 'Unmanned Aerial Vehicles (UAVs): An Assessment of Historical Operations and Future Possibilities', unpublished research paper, ACSC, Maxwell Air Force Base, 1997, pp.8-13.

[22] Armitage, pp.66-69.

[23] McDaid, H. and Oliver, D. *Robot Warriors* (Orion Media, 1997), pp.38-39; Armitage, pp.70-71.

[24] McDaid and Oliver, p.38; Armitage, p.71.

[25] Tilford, E. *Set Up: What the Air Force Did in Vietnam and Why* (Air University Press, Maxwell Air Force Base, 1991), Chap. 3; Armitage, pp.74-75, 81.

[26] Armitage, p.76.

[27] Jones, C. *op. cit.*, pp. 8-11; Armitage, pp.76-78.

[28] Armitage, pp.78-81.

[29] **www.pbs.org-NOVA** (July 2008); Jones, p.17.

[30] **www.pbs.org-NOVA** (July 2008); Armitage, pp.82-86.

[31] For example, it was suggested in a US Department of Defence study, entitled 'Unmanned Aerial Vehicles and Uninhabited Combat Aerial Vehicles', dated February 2004 (p.3), that acceptance of UAVs and recognition of their worth has always been slow, and that proper conceptualisation of unmanned systems has occurred only within the last five or six years.

UNMANNED AERIAL VEHICLE OPERATIONS SINCE
THE 1980s

Dr David Jordan & Ben Wilkins

The successful employment of unmanned aerial vehicles (Uavs) in Vietnam did not lead to their widespread acceptance within the United States, or in many other nations. While there was a clear appreciation of the value that could be gained from utilising unmanned systems for battlefield observation – perhaps best exemplified in NATO by the Canadair CL-89 and its derivatives – there was a general lack of impetus in taking forward the technologies underpinning Uavs. Although aviation journals – often those aimed at enthusiasts – sometimes speculated on air power becoming dominated by aircraft controlled remotely by pilots sitting in the relative comfort of control bunkers, a variety of factors militated against the widespread development of Uavs for the remaining years of the Cold War. However, within only a few years of the collapse of the Soviet Union, unmanned aerial vehicles were deployed on combat operations, gathering vital intelligence information; and a less than a decade beyond that, Uavs carrying weapons were to be found playing a notable part in operations in a variety of locations around the world. This chapter traces the somewhat rocky development of Uavs over the course of the past quarter-century, where the UAV has moved from being an idea in search of support and proper management to playing a significant part in military operations around the globe.

As the Cold War drew to a close in the late 1980s, the prospects for the future use of UAV by armed services were not altogether clear. Although what were then referred to as Remotely Piloted Vehicles (RPVs) had been used with some success in the Vietnam War, there had been a certain loss of enthusiasm in the United States during the latter part of the 1970s. In 1975, the position had been very different – the US Air Force had been carrying out trials which saw RPVs carrying precision weapons and electronic warfare systems, in a bid to evaluate expanding their role from reconnaissance. Within twelve months, however, the picture had changed. Control of RPVs passed from Strategic Air Command to Tactical Air Command (TAC). As TAC was on the verge of procuring large numbers of A-10s and F-16s, this placed considerable funding pressure on UAV projects; by 1978, the last operational USAF RPV squadron was disbanded, and all but one American RPV/UAV programmes had been abandoned by 1981, only the Army's Aquila mini-UAV remaining – and even this system ultimately failed to enter service.[1] There were also signs of institutional resistance to the idea of new technology, with the Government Accountability Office noting in 1981 that 'RPVs appear to suffer from the attitude of the users and not from technological drawbacks or infeasible systems.'[2]

While interest in Uavs appeared to have waned in the United States, the same could not be said of Israel, where the development of unmanned systems had been a source of considerable interest since the 1973 Yom Kippur/October War. RPVs offered a means by which the relative small Israeli Defence Force (IDF) could expand reconnaissance capability without the need to expand its RF-4 Phantom fleet (at considerably greater cost), while also offering the opportunity to conduct operations where the risk of losing airframes was high without the concomitant loss of aircrew.[3] By 1982, the IDF had a mixture of RPVs which it went on to use to great effect in the Lebanon War of that year. The IDF's planning relied upon detailed information of enemy dispositions, much of which was obtained by a combination of manned and unmanned aerial platforms. The location of almost every Syrian radar and surface to air missile (SAM) site in the Bekka valley was discovered, and even the mobility of some of the SAM systems was offset by regular and persistent overflight, which allowed maps to be updated to the extent that information about the Syrian ground based air defences was no more than 48 hours old.[4]

RPVs were also employed in the Israeli Suppression of Enemy Air Defences (SEAD) effort which opened the Bekaa Valley campaign, being used to encourage Syrian SAM radars to come on air. Once they were emitting and located, the radars were attacked by manned aircraft and the missile batteries themselves, useless without radar guidance, bombed.[5] RPVs were not only used as decoys in the campaign to destroy the Syrian air defence system; there is evidence that Mastiff RPVs provided electronic intelligence which allowed IDF Boeing 707s converted for use in the electronic countermeasures role to respond quickly when the Syrians attempted to exploit the relatively limited frequency agility of SAMs such as the SA-6.[6] The RPVs conducted post-strike reconnaissance, and their contribution to the IDF's success in the opening stage of what evolved into a long and seemingly interminable insurgency was judged by some observers to be 'one of the most important lessons of the war'.[7]

RPVs were utilised not only at the operational level, but with tactical-level formations such as artillery command posts to improve the situational awareness and responsiveness of their guns. Coordinates of enemy positions were obtained from the RPV systems, and this allowed rapid dissemination of the exact location of target sets to the gun batteries, which were often able to engage targets which might otherwise have relied upon their mobility to evade destruction. The value of RPVs was not lost on senior Israeli commanders and politicians; the then-Defence Minister, Ariel Sharon, later claimed that he had watched the evacuation of PLO positions in Beirut via an RPV.[8]

The success of the employment of RPVs by the Israelis sparked new interest in the United States, both within the individual armed services and the Department of Defense. The successful and innovative employment of small, low-technology and relatively low-cost systems against some of the Soviet air defence systems likely to be encountered in Europe by NATO in the event of war suggested that it would be profitable to resume exploration of unmanned aerial technology. The possibility that relatively low-cost platforms which were relatively easy to replace if lost, and whose loss would incur no human casualties could offset the numerical superiority of the Warsaw Pact became a notion that entered the minds of aviation authors as well as senior officers in the US. As it transpired, the unmanned aerial vehicle would prove to be rather more sophisticated and expensive than some of the optimistic projections of the early 1980s suggested.

A further influence upon the renewed interest in UAVs in the US came about as a result of what might be regarded as fortuitous timing. At about the same time as Israeli UAVs were proving their viability over the Bekaa Valley, the American Defense Advanced Research Projects Agency (DARPA) had begun to examine the idea of long-endurance UAVs, partly because the agency had recently ceased to manage 'stealth' programmes such as the F-117, and this newly-released capacity was free to explore new concepts and projects that appeared to be of value; more cynically, some observers suggest that DARPA had 'an almost subconscious motive: to find the next stealth'.[9] While DARPA began exploring the potential of marrying long endurance UAVs with new technologies – ranging from solar power to synthetic aperture radar – the Israelis continued to develop a series of smaller, more tactically-focused platforms to build upon the successes of 1982.

The 1980s thus saw a notable increase in development of unmanned aerial platforms, although DARPA's programmes were frequently hidden from wider view by security issues. A series of projects investigating the technologies of long-endurance UAVs followed. In 1984, DARPA embarked upon the complementary Project Amber, intended to develop a series of smaller UAVs. The contract for project development was given to a small company, Leading Systems, (which literally began life in the garage of its founder's house). By late 1986, Leading Systems had produced six prototypes – three UAVs for reconnaissance purposes and three more which were designed to serve as loitering cruise missiles.[10] Alongside development of the project Amber airframes, Leading Systems also created a simpler derivative known as the Gnat 750.

Although DARPA's UAV projects demonstrated considerable promise, by the late 1980s, none of them appeared likely to produce a platform or platforms which would soon be in service. In 1986, the Senate Appropriations Committee expressed serious concerns over the apparent lack of direction inherent in the services' approach to UAVs, and directed the DoD to produce a so-called 'master plan' for UAVs to be considered at hearings for the Fiscal Year 1988 defence budget. This did not occur, and Congress produced a sharply worded commentary which accused the services of 'pursuing programs and technologies that should be merged to avoid duplication and to ensure cost effective approaches'. It imposed funding constraints on UAV development, mandating that work on unmanned systems should be conducted on a joint basis. Release of funds even for joint programmes was not authorised until the 'master plan' had been submitted.[11] When the plan finally arrived before Congress, in June 1988, the Government Accounting Office noted that it did not remove duplication of platforms across the services, and sought to delay joint acquisition projects until 1990. It also discovered that a supposedly joint project in which the US Navy had responsibility for development of the UAV airframe and the USAF the sensor payload had seen the Navy develop its own payload for the system, claiming that its sensor system would be ready for use earlier, more effective and cheaper than that being developed by the USAF.

However, as the GAO noted, such a claim was problematic, since the Navy had failed to conduct any testing which would validate its claims for greater effectiveness, while the service entry dates for both payloads were the same – the claim for earlier availability was measured in, at most, a few months.[12] Congress was unamused.

As a result of Congressional irritation, a new authority for all US military UAVs, the Joint Program Office (JPO) was established. The JPO rationalised the variety of projects underway at the time seeking to focus upon a short-range UAV for the Army, and a joint USAF/US Navy system which was to be a medium-range, high-speed platform capable of being launched from an aircraft or a shipboard ramp. Unfortunately, the JPO complicated matters by concluding that further research and development into UAVs should be undertaken by industry. The number of UAVs required by the US armed services at that time was insufficient to interest the major defence companies, and while smaller firms were interested, they lacked the capital to conduct the level of research and development necessary. Compounding matters, Congress mandated that the JPO was the sole authority on UAV technologies and would set spending priorities. DARPA and the individual services were not permitted to spend on UAVs unless directed to do so by the JPO. As a result, there was no money for research and development, and the smaller concerns which had been interested in the field turned their attention elsewhere. The JPO had been intended to expedite UAV technologies – but, by the early 1990s, it had actually retarded development.[13]

Congressional interest in the development of UAVs came against a background of growing interest in such systems amongst the services. The US Navy became particularly keen to obtain its own unmanned aerial vehicles after the debacle of its involvement in Lebanon in late 1983. USN aircraft supporting the United Nations peacekeeping mission to Lebanon were targeted by Syrian ground fire on a number of occasions, prompting a retaliatory strike against anti-aircraft positions on 4 December 1983. The attack led to the loss of two US Navy aircraft (an A-7 Corsair and an A-6 Intruder), and the death of the A-6 pilot and the incarceration of his bombardier-navigator, who was released only when the Syrians negotiated with the would-be Democratic presidential candidate, Senator Jesse Jackson, having pointedly refused to have any discussions with the Reagan administration. The political complications caused by the capture of US service personnel became apparent.[14]

Ten days after the air strikes, the battleship USS *New Jersey* bombarded suspected anti-aircraft positions, but to little effect as locating the targets was difficult (without placing manned reconnaissance aircraft at risk), and battle damage assessment was similarly problematic. The difficulties encountered during the Lebanon operation prompted the then-Secretary of the Navy, John Lehman, to direct the to invest in off-the shelf systems for operational testing.[15] Since there were no readily-available American systems, the Navy turned to Israel, procuring a number of Malat Mastiff III RPVs. The US Marine Corps' first RPV platoon was established in June 1984 to operate the Mastiffs. Another RPV based on an Israeli design, the RQ-2 Pioneer joined the USN in 1986, and the USMC received three similar systems (each Pioneer system including eight aerial vehicles) in 1987.

The US Army, meanwhile, had been pursuing its own UAV, the Lockheed MQM-105 Aquila. This had its origins in the early 1970s, as part of the Target Acquisition, Designation and Aerial Reconnaissance (TADAR) programme, which was intended to provide a lightweight, low-cost battlefield observation system. The test programme in 1982 was afflicted by serious issues regarding systems integration. The plan to have no fewer than 995 MQM-105s in service by 1985 was clearly too optimistic, as was the desired sensor fit. As the manufacturers struggled to provide sensors for the Aquila, costs quintupled. After spending more than $1 billion on the project, it became clear that the Aquila could not be made to work without incurring disproportionate costs, and it was cancelled in 1987.[16] The Army instead joined the Pioneer procurement, obtaining a single system, which arrived for testing in 1990.

The USAF, meanwhile, had tested a number of UAV, but none reached operational service. Thus, as the Cold War drew to a close, none of the US services had a robust UAV capability, even though the value of such systems had been identified more than 20 years before. However, these disappointments came against the background of growing enthusiasm for unmanned platforms; the Reagan administration's Fiscal Year 1987 budget requested greater funding for unmanned systems, marking the point at which the United States began the move from being in possession of an array of experimental programmes which had not led to the fielding of operational systems to the procurement of unmanned aerial vehicles intended for use by the armed services.[17]

It became clear that the tardy and disorganised development of UAVs prior to the FY 1987 budget request had denied the US forces an extremely useful intelligence-gathering capability when the lessons learned, on 2 August 1990, Saddam Hussein invaded Kuwait, culminating in the formation of an international coalition to evict Iraq from Kuwaiti territory by force if necessary. Saddam ignored UN mandates, and by the end of the year, it was clear that it would not be long before military operations to achieve this goal began. While the subsequent war was a resounding military victory for the US-led coalition, the role played by UAVs was rather less than it might have been had the disorganised and often half-hearted approach of the previous decade been avoided.

Operation Desert Storm

Although events in Lebanon had pushed forward American interest in the development of UAVs, even the off-the-shelf procurement of Pioneers had done little to provide the level of UAV coverage that was desired. Only 50 were in the inventory when hostilities began. The US Army had only recently acquired its system, and this was undertaking a number of tests when the need to deploy became clear. The end result was that the Army's Pioneer platoon did not arrive in theatre until a week after hostilities broke out, and it did not fly a mission until 1 February 1991.[18] The few air vehicles available were assigned to US VII Corps, and performed extremely well – however, once the quality of information which could be obtained from the systems became apparent, there were requests for UAV coverage from the Corps staff which were simply impossible to provide because of the lack of airframes available.

The few Pioneers available managed to provide valuable intelligence about enemy positions, and delivered information about so many targets that it was impossible for VII Corps to make plans to attack all of them. Cordesman and Wagner suggest 'a relatively cheap and simple UAV provided far more useful manoeuvre and firepower allocation data than any possible combination of billions of dollars worth of satellites and manned fixed-wing assets'.[19]

The USMC enjoyed similar levels of success with the four Pioneer companies which it deployed during the war. 138 missions were flown during the build up to the conflict, while another 185 missions were carried out during the fighting itself. As it became clear that the information provided by the Pioneers was vital to the planning and prosecution of the USMC's operations, efforts were made to bring as many Pioneers as possible into theatre, sourcing additional resources from developmental establishments.

Similar value from the Pioneers was obtained by the USN. Perhaps the best example of the effectiveness of the Pioneer in meeting its originally-intended task of enhancing the accuracy of naval gunfire support was provided by one of the most peculiar incidents of the war. One of these UAVs, launched from the battleship USS *Wisconsin*, became uncontrollable and headed off over Iraqi positions on Faylaka Island, which had already been subjected to heavy bombardment by the *Wisconsin* and its sister-ship, the USS *Missouri*. The operators were astounded to see enemy troops pouring out of their bunkers and trenches waving any white material they could lay their hands upon in a desperate bid to surrender prior – they assumed – to the arrival of yet more 16-inch shells from the battleships. One account has it that the Pioneer operators had lost flight control over the UAV, and that after a while, adding to the impression that the little UAV had developed a mind of its own, the Pioneer seemed to tire of the situation and flew off, later crashing when it ran out of fuel.[20]

Desert Storm confirmed the utility of UAVs once more, and while the claim made by one author that 'the UAV came of age during Operation Desert Shield/

Desert Storm' rather overlooks the importance of Israeli operations in Lebanon, it is not unfair to suggest that events in the Persian Gulf in 1991 reinforced the view in the United States that there was a need for an increased UAV capability.[21] After-action assessments were less than favourable in their views on the approach taken by all three services to UAVs prior to 1991.

Anthony Cordesman and Abraham Wagner pulled no punches in outlining the reason for this state of affairs:

> One of the reasons the US Army lacked effective tactical intelligence support in Desert Storm was that it had mismanaged its development of UAVs during the preceding decade. The failure of ...the Aquila program was only part of a much broader failure to develop a family of sensors, develop advanced packages of sensors, and an adequate data transmission system. The Army's failures in this area are widely regarded as one of the worst examples of overall program management and development activity in US military history.[22]

Cordesman and Wagner were hardly more complimentary about the other services, noting that the USMC did not have enough systems, while the focus of the USAF upon strategic UAV programmes which had failed to deliver the sort of capability required for battlefield use meant that they had little to offer. In spite of the relatively basic nature of the UAVs available at the time, the amount of information which could be obtained suggested that the ability to provide real-time or near real-time data to commanders at formation level gave the US forces benefitting from the provision of this intelligence an additional edge. The Pioneers suffered few losses to enemy fire, and the level of persistence over the battlefield offered by the type was notable, although the implications of this long-term loitering ability were perhaps not fully appreciated at the time.

Cordesman and Wagner lamented the fact that there had been no real debate over the value of the UAV in modern warfare, or over the need for more capable systems with longer range.[23] In fact, the recognition of just how useful UAVs might be had occurred, and there was little need for real debate – it was not a question of whether UAVs were useful and should be procured, rather one of how such systems should be procured and used. The US armed forces were forced to return to the tangled remnants of indigenous UAV procurement polity in a bid to set out a path ahead. As the author Bill Yenne observed, 'it was not until the mid-1990s that the promise and potential of UAVs had progressed to the point where they could be considered to be fully integrated in American military doctrine'.[24]

Building UAV capability after Desert Storm

With a further illustration of the clear benefits that could be gained from UAVs, the general lack of progress within the US procurement system became a source of growing concern within the American defence community, even though it was felt by some observers that more traditionalist interests in the air force and navy were far from unhappy at the slow rate of development. The JPO was seen as an obstacle to progress, and revelations by the GAO of high spending on UAV projects with only the problematic BQM/AQM-145 medium range UAV and the army's Hunter short-range UAV to show for it. Informed observers were unsurprised when the JPO was, to all intents and purposes, abandoned when it was subsumed into the Defense Airborne Reconnaissance Office (DARO), formed in 1994.[25]

DARO took over just one active UAV programme, the Gnat-750, which, after the failure of the original design authority, Leading Systems, had been acquired by General Atomics. A number of Gnat-750s and their ground stations were soon ordered by the Central Intelligence Agency's (CIA) Directorate of Science and Technology. Beyond the auspices of the Pentagon, the CIA was not bound by the restrictions placed on UAV procurement by Congress, and pressed ahead with the project. A number of Gnat-750s were deployed in 1994, first to Albania, and then to a still-publically undisclosed location, believed to be Hungary. Although weather conditions are thought to have adversely affected the Gant-750's performance during the first deployment, the results of the second overseas operation were encouraging.[26]

This performance appears to have helped to contribute to the Gnat-750's selection as part of DARO's first major project, which was another attempt at a long endurance UAV. To reduce risk, DARO decided that it would divide the programme into two 'tiers', with Gnat-750 serving as the 'Tier I' UAV. An evolution of the Gnat-750, built by General Atomics' Aeronautical Systems Inc division would form Tier II – this was to be known as the Predator. The next step, Tier II+ , would be fulfilled by a type capable of loitering at altitudes of up to 65,000 feet for 24 hours at a range of almost 3,500 miles from its home base.

The competition to provide the Tier II+ and Tier III capabilities was fiercer than anticipated, but culminated with Teledyne Ryan being given the contract to produce what would become the RQ-4 Global Hawk. The impressive RQ-4 was soon overshadowed by the emergence of the Tier III platform, the RQ-3 DarkStar [sic], produced by an alliance between Boeing and Lockheed Martin, and which attracted considerable attention for its unusual appearance:

> It was so unusual that the trade publication *Defense News*, which acquired a leaked drawing of the aircraft before the roll-out, helpfully added an arrow to indicate the direction of flight – and got it backwards. Even one Lockheed Martin company publication printed a photo of the vehicle upside down.[27]

DarkStar first flew in March 1996, but on its second flight, it crashed, and the entire programme came to a halt. The Global Hawk programme continued, first flying in 1998. These two new and technologically impressive programmes rather overshadowed the fact that the simpler Predator, had already entered USAF service. The 11th Reconnaissance Squadron activated in July 1995, receiving ten Advanced Concept Technology Demonstration airframes.

Several were deployed to the Balkans to support United Nations operations over the former Yugoslavia between July 1995 and March 1996. A month after the return of the demonstration Predators to the United States, the USAF was confirmed as the operating service for the Predator, receiving production airframes from 1997.

While Predator numbers increased, the promise shown by the Global Hawk led to the withdrawal of funding for DarkStar in early 1999. DARO also disappeared as part of the Defense Reform Initiative. There had been some criticism of DARO's handling of UAV development which helped contribute to this decision, although some observers later questioned whether or not all of the criticism had been deserved.[28]

While the bureaucratic progression of UAV management turned in yet another direction, the actual deployment of American UAVs on operations in the Balkans may, perhaps, be seen as the point at which the value of employing unmanned systems finally began to be given greater credence. The ability of UAVs to provide reconnaissance information regarding activities by the warring parties in the Balkans had been demonstrated to good effect, despite the fact that UAVs were less robust than manned aircraft. UAVs offered major advantages in terms of their ability to loiter relatively unobtrusively over areas of interest for long periods, and because of the fact that the loss of an unmanned airframe was far less politically loaded than suffering attrition amongst manned aircraft; the loss of the F-16 piloted by Captain Scott O'Grady to a Serbian surface to air missile in June 1995 and the subsequent public reaction to his recovery illustrated just how greatly reduced the political risks of employing unmanned platforms might be (although it should be noted that the sortie O'Grady was flying was to maintain the UN No-Fly Zone over Bosnia, which was not a task a UAV could undertake).

Although relatively limited, the role played by the Predator system sent to the Balkans in 1995 was worthy of note. As the Director of DARO noted:

> In July 1995, a Predator system was deployed to Albania to support Joint Task Force (JTF) Provide Promise. I hat deployment clearly demonstrated the potential of UAVs to support military forces by monitoring civilian activities, troop locations, artillery positions, garrison activities, and compliance with agreements. Predator was instrumental in verifying that Bosnians were not complying with agreements to garrison their forces. When air forces were employed in Deliberate Force, Predator was used for real time targeting and retargeting. As a result of the Deliberate Force operation, Bosnian compliance was achieved and the Dayton Peace Accord was signed by all parties.[29]

The further deployment to Hungary in 1996 in support of operations by the UN Implementation Force (IFOR) and then the Stabilisation Force (SFOR) which maintained the terms of the Dayton Accords proved successful, although as already noted weather was an issue for UAV operations. Just as with the Gnat-750s, the harsh winter created serious problems for the Predators, and this led to moves to introduce a de-icing capability on two specially modified air vehicles. Unfortunately, the weather proved so inclement that neither was able to fly.[30]

However, the inherent value of the Predator was appreciated, and when the next stage in the Balkan conflicts played out in Kosovo, the fact that UAVs would be of considerable utility was fully appreciated. As the situation in Kosovo deteriorated, the international community attempted to bring about a diplomatic solution to the crisis, but this could not be achieved. As a result, the NATO member nations concluded - with considerable reluctance on the part of some – that it would be necessary to carry out coercive air attacks on the Yugoslavia in a bid to bring President Slobodan Milosevic's compliance with the terms of the Rambouillet agreement which attempted to bring about a settlement to the crisis.[31]

Operation Allied Force – Kosovo, 1999

In the build-up to Operation Allied Force, the diplomatic manoeuvring that occurred as the Organisation for Security and Cooperation in Europe (OSCE) endeavoured to monitor events in Kosovo saw the deployment of a number of USAF Predators, flying from Hungary in a bid to provide the OSCE with as much information as possible on events in the disputed province. The Predators conducted a number of overflights during October and November 1998, but had to be withdrawn and replaced by CL-289 UAVs operated by the German army during the winter as a result of icing problems which militated against the Predators flying.[32] The CL-289s, operating from Macedonia, were still in place when the decision to coerce President Milosevic's regime by air attack was taken.

Predictions that Milosevic would be forced to the negotiating table after a few days of bombing proved ill-founded, and the need for additional ISTAR assets became obvious. There had been no attempt to deploy Predators to the Balkans again, not least because the USAF was concerned over the fact that the technical manuals for the type had not been validated, an issue which had led to delays in the Initial Operational Testing and Evaluation programme.[33] The requirement for additional ISTAR assets overrode these concerns, and it was not long before elements of the 11th Reconnaissance Squadron had been despatched to support operations in the Balkans. They were joined by US Navy RQ-2A Pioneers, which were to be used to locate targets for attack by naval aircraft (most notably P-3 Orions using the AGM-84E Stand-off Land Attack Missile) and to maintain a watch on Yugoslavian naval units based in Montenegro. The German army reinforced its CL-289 battery that was already in place. The French army sent a number of its CL-289s, while the British prepared to deploy the much-lampooned Phoenix UAV system, operated by the Royal Artillery.[34] The US Army also despatched UAVs, in the form of the recently-rejuvenated RQ-5 Hunter, which had enjoyed a new lease of life after improvements to components which had been responsible for a spate of crashes in 1995. The first Hunter mission was conducted on 4 April 1999.

Used as a means of providing real-time surveillance of tactical targets such as artillery positions and Yugoslavian army positions, Hunter imagery was downlinked to Skopje, and then sent on either to NATO headquarters, the Combined Air Operations Centre (CAOC) in Belgium, or direct to the Pentagon. The targets of interest for the Hunters were frequently well-defended, with half of the eight losses sustained by the type being to surface-to-air missiles.[35]

Although the air campaign lasted rather longer than envisaged, the part played by UAVs was notable in terms of the contribution made to ISTAR. It may not be unreasonable to suggest that as far as the United States and the United Kingdom were concerned, Operation Allied Force marked the point at which it became clear that UAVs were valuable force multipliers which had to be brought into much more widespread use than had been the case before (the Israelis, of course, had reached this conclusion over fifteen years previously).

After a delay in getting the Predators ready for operations, they proved particularly successful in the location of Yugoslav army formations, which allowed NATO attack aircraft to be sent in to engage these targets before they dispersed or moved on to new locations. NATO's UAVs were also put to work conducting Battle Damage Assessment (BDA), but despite the best efforts of the UAV operators, the overall BDA coverage was later felt to have fallen short of the ideal.[36]

Nevertheless, the work of the UAVs available was noted for its general efficacy, even though Predator and Hunter were both found to be in need of better optical sensors if they were to provide effective imagery from heights above 8,000 feet.[37] The British Phoenix system fared rather better, even though it was employed for tasks it was not designed for:

> On the D-day when they crossed over, the Phoenix detected 12 Mig 21s at Pristina as the Serbs were withdrawing, these were detected at some considerable range. It is interesting that a previous RPV had flown over the same location and had not located that, it had declared the area clear. It has a much better resolution than comparable systems. Now when the Russians occupied the airport the Phoenix overflew the complete area and was able to identify vehicles and give information on their activity. Because of the low cloud in that area, Phoenix was often the only UAV in theatre that was able to provide any information on a regular basis. It was tasked with monitoring the ground security zone and it did that effectively. Prior to D-day it conducted a search of all known Serb positions and this proved in fact in the majority of cases the Serbs had withdrawn. It gave our forces a tremendous capability which we did not have before.[38]

While the Phoenix provided much useful information, it did so at a high cost in airframes, with 13 being lost during both the campaign and the aftermath where the platform was in use to monitor Serb compliance with the peace agreement which had brought Allied Force to a conclusion. By the time the Select Committee on Defence report on Kosovo had been published, a number of UAV programmes for the British forces were in place, most notably the move to replace Phoenix with the Watchkeeper system.[39]

The success of UAVs encouraged the Americans to give even greater consideration to the fielding of such systems. The fusing of imagery from Predators with information obtained from E-8C Joint STARS surveillance aircraft greatly enhanced USAF targeting options. However, this added a further complication in that it soon became clear that employing Predators to cue attack aircraft demanded that the operators of the system be trained in the arts of forward air control. As Secretary of the Air Force James Roche recalled in 2003:

> When we first fielded the Predator, the intelligence community owned it. So in Kosovo, when the Predator found Serb forces in a village there, we d have one of those frustrating, yet predictable conversations as we tried to come up with ways to make these new systems work for the warfighters. When they'd see a tank between two red-roofed buildings, the Predator pilot or systems operator would try to talk the eyes of the A-10 pilot onto the tank. But the people flying the Predator were not people who were schooled in close air support or the tactics of forward air control.[40]

This problem was quickly addressed thanks to the intervention of the Commander of US Air Forces in Europe, General John P Jumper:

> So, as [General] John [Jumper] likes to tell it, you'd have this "dialogue of the deaf" between the Predator crew and the A-10 crew: "Sir, it's the tank between the two red roofed buildings." Of course, the A-10 sees 40 villages all with red roofs. The operator of the Predator is looking through a soda straw at 10-power magnification. He says, Well, if you look over to the left there's a road right beside the two houses. A tree line is right next to that. A river is running nearby ..." Forty-five minutes later, the A-10 might be in the same Zip code, but certainly hasn't gotten his or her eyes on the target.

> After too many of these exasperating exchanges, John said, "let's put a laser designator on the Predator." The rapid reaction part of the acquisition community came in and did just that. It took them just two weeks to put a laser designation device on the Predator. Then, we quickly learned how to do target designation and talk others onto a target.[41]

Jumper's intervention led to the procurement of a number of Raytheon AAS-44 sensor systems, which contained a laser ranger and a laser designator. This provided Predator operators with the ability to designate targets directly for suitably armed attack aircraft. The capability arrived just too late to see use, but proved effective when tested in the United States after the air campaign had finished. Had the campaign continued, it had been intended to send the Predators below the cloud base to locate and designate targets for attack aircraft, which were not permitted to descend to the altitudes necessary to bring them out under the clouds, even though this meant that their laser-guided weapons could not be employed. The decision to bar low level operations had been taken in a bid to ensure that NATO casualties were minimised, but this compromised the effectiveness of the air operations; although the use of UAVs with suitable designation equipment offered one solution to the problem, the US also chose to pursue the development of weapons guided through the use of the Global Positioning System, leading to the creation of the all-weather Joint Direct Attack Munition (JDAM) series of bombs, a solution followed by the RAF with the decision to introduce a GPS-capability on its Enhanced Paveway series of bombs.

Once Allied Force came to an end, the prospect of employing Predators for designation purposes faced a notable threat:

> [T]he tyranny of our acquisition process engaged again, and that laser designator came off the aircraft because it wasn't "in the program".[42]

General Jumper, who moved from his post in Europe to become chief of USAF Air Combat Command in February 2000, soon discovered that the upgraded sensor systems had been removed, and directed that they should be put back again. He also made a decisive contribution to the way in which Predator would be employed in future, by calling for Predator to be fitted with a weapon – as the aircraft had a laser designator Jumper reasoned that it was folly for the Predators not to carry laser-guided weapons of their own, in the form of the AGM-114 Hellfire anti-armour missile. Jumper was told that such a project would take five years to implement and cost around $15 million. Unimpressed, Jumper gave the project team $3 million and three months to conduct preliminary testing.[43] Jumper's timeline was met, giving the Predator a significant capability which will be discussed further below.

Although the ability to use Predator as a targeting system was one of the positive outcomes from Allied Force, another issue arose, namely that of the presence of a system which could provide real-time imagery being misapplied by commanders seeking to employ a 'long screwdriver' approach to operations. The most notable offender appears to have been General Clark himself, as according to officers working in the CAOC:

> [General Clark] would on occasions telephone the CAOC demanding that UAVs break off from their tasking and go and look at things of interest to him. Clark was in daily telephone contact with Kosovo Liberation Army chief, Hashim Thaci, and immediately after these conversations would dispatch a UAV to look at what often turned out to be spurious targets.[44]

This presented a number of difficulties, since a number of airmen argued that SACEUR's intervention in the tasking process meant that a number of critical targets, carefully chosen by the intelligence community as being worthy of further examination went without coverage as a result; furthermore, some suggested that Clark occasionally succumbed to a temptation to micro-manage based upon what he could see from UAV feed, forgetting that his view was that of a man 'looking through a soda straw at 10-power magnification'. This hazard was outweighed by the value of the imagery that could be provided by UAVs, although the dangers of a commander demanding so much coverage that the apportionment of assets became a live issue which remains to be resolved.

Perhaps the most important aspect of UAVs in Allied Force, however, was the fact that it was obvious that the value they added to operations was substantial, even if there were some limitations arising from technology and procedural issues that arose:

> UAVs such as USAF Predator and US Army Hunter could identify targets through their real time video output. Limits on the efficient use of UAVs during Allied Force were due mostly to the lack of integration with the conventional operational forces. UAVs had never been integrated into the air tasking order (ATO) with strike packages and the lack of training between UAVs and FACAs made tasks such as altitude deconfliction and target talk-ons difficult. Even so, the ability of UAVs to locate and identify Serbian forces was a much sought after capability and operational techniques were quickly patched together. One example was the effort to connect Predator with the FACA. A Tactical Air Control Party (TACP) controller located at the CAOC, monitored Predator video and performed real time target talk-ons via a radio link through the Airborne Command and Control Center (ABCCC) to FACAs overflying the target area. The occasions when these missions were successful provided a glimpse into the potential of fully integrated UAV platforms with conventional strike aircraft. But UAV-FACA employment techniques were in their infancy at the end of Allied Force and did not produce a significant number of target engagements.[45]

After Allied Force

Whatever the issues raised by the access commanders could gain from footage provided by UAVs, the Kosovo campaign could be said to have marked a turning point for the widespread use of UAVs. Although Predator gained most of the publicity, the work done by the differing systems employed illustrated that the UAV offered an enormously beneficial increase in ISTAR capability if employed correctly; the ability to cue strike aircraft against targets was also a powerfully seductive prospect for air operations planners.

The ability to cue 'shooters' against targets was not all that emerged from the lessons identified form Allied Force. The experience only reinforced General Jumper's view that the next logical step was to fit the craft themselves with armament was a timely one. The lessons of Kosovo were identified and digested against a backdrop of militaries – particularly in the United States

- considering the way in which technological transformation might render their operations more effective. Amongst the discussions underpinning these broad concepts lay the idea of reducing the time in the 'kill chain' by improving 'sensor-to-shooter' links, to which UAV operations over Kosovo had given added impetus. Jumper's directive that the USAF's Predators should be given the ability to carry their own weapons represented the ultimate logical conclusion to the desire to compress the links between 'sensor' and 'shooter' through the elegant expedient of making the sensor itself into the shooter so that it could deal with time sensitive target sets which required engaging immediately, rather than waiting for manned platforms to be sent to attack. By early 2001, test launches of Hellfire missiles from Predator had gone well.

Development of the Global Hawk had also progressed satisfactorily. In late 2000, it had been suggested that the pace of Global Hawk development should be increased by the expedient of diverting funds from the U-2 programme; the USAF decided against increasing the pace of the U-2's retirement to the extent that the proposal suggested, but it became clear that the Global Hawk's capabilities were likely to make it the long-term replacement for the reconnaissance aircraft.[46]

The arrival of Donald Rumsfeld at the Pentagon as part of President George W Bush's first administration meant that the issue of transformation was high on the political agenda from the outset, and the terrorist attacks on the World Trade Center on 9 September 2001 created a situation where Rumsfeld's vision of a much 'lighter' US military drawing heavily upon technology came to be tested on operations far earlier than might otherwise have been the case. As UAVs were amongst the systems at the cutting edge of transformational technology, it should be no surprise that the intervention in Afghanistan and the subsequent US-led invasion of Iraq saw UAVs come into their own.

Uavs and 'the War on Terror'

The attacks by Al Qaeda on 11 September 2001 transformed not only the global strategic context, but helped to drive forward the widespread employment of unmanned aerial vehicles. Far removed from the early reluctance to engage with unmanned technology in the 1980s, the United States has been at the forefront of operational developments and deployments. The Israeli Defence Forces have continued to exploit their unmanned aerial systems, and a number of 'new' players have materialised. The Italian Air Force has obtained and deployed Predators, while Britain has become an enthusiastic proponent of UAVs, employing them alongside the Americans in both Afghanistan and Iraq – literally alongside, because of the establishment of the Joint Predator Task Force (JPTF), within the 57th Operations Wing at Nellis AFB containing both British and American personnel.

On 7 October 2001, the United States began operations against Afghanistan. The opening phase of operations relied heavily upon special operations forces, in conjunction with air power. Working in conjunction with AC-130s gunships, Predators were used to send information across to the 'shooter' as it approached the target, allowing the crew to orientate much more quickly, allowing swifter engagement of the enemy.[47] The armed Predators, although equipped to tackle what General Jumper referred to as 'fleeting and perishable targets', caused some confusion amongst legal advisors attempting to reconcile the rules of engagement (ROE) with the employment of ordnance released by operators thousands of miles from the battlefield.[48] This allegedly led to some high-value targets not being struck until the ROE were made more permissive.[49] Operation Enduring Freedom also saw the Global Hawk in use, with its ability to remain aloft above a battlefield for hours at a time making it an invaluable tool, providing real time information of the kind commanders have sought for centuries.

By the time of the invasion of Iraq in March 2003, the importance of UAVs to operations was firmly established. While the destruction of an Iraqi ZSU-23-4 self-propelled anti-aircraft gun near al-Amarah by a Hellfire launched by a Predator attracted press attention, the work of ISTAR UAVs tended to go unnoticed. Yet again, however, the scale of information that could be obtained from the unmanned platforms provided commanders with the ability to make informed decisions based upon near-real time or real time reconnaissance product. Even when the advance into Iraq was held up by fierce sandstorms, use of Global Hawks flying well above or offset from the storms enabled a constant stream of intelligence to be provided, ensuring that coalition commanders were not left making educated guesses based upon a mixture of partial information, experience and instinct.

Although the Taleban and Saddam Hussein were removed from power, the enduring nature of operations in both Afghanistan and Iraq provided plenty of opportunities for the unique characteristics of UAVs to come to the fore. The value of aircraft in providing overwatch in low intensity conflicts, giving advanced warning of ambushes or obstacles along the route of a convoy, had been proven years before, and it was natural to turn the Predator to this task.[50] Its small size, low noise signature and ability to loiter gave it a considerable advantage over manned aircraft, while the ability to strike targets immediately ensured that the enemy was unable to enjoy a window of opportunity as air support was despatched. UAV surveillance also came to play a part in the effort to reduce the threat posed by insurgent improvised explosive devices, which have become a favoured weapon both in Iraq and Afghanistan.

The ability of UAVs to provide a detailed picture of an area of interest thanks to constant surveillance represented a major change in the way in which air power could support counter-insurgency operations; it also represents a profound change in the characteristics of air power itself – a platform able to loiter over a battlespace for up to twenty-four hours at a time mitigates one of the profound limitations of air power, namely impermanence. It is not impossible to envisage this level of persistence expanding as more capable armed UAVs enter service, providing the ability to garner information over an extended period of time, while being able to carry out time-sensitive attacks on targets of opportunity.

If evidence of how attitudes to UAVs have altered over the last quarter century were required, it is perhaps worth noting that the American Predator fleet reached 100,000 hours during a routine patrol over Iraq in September 2004, with 70 per cent of those hours being achieved on operational taskings.[51] Furthermore, since 1999, Britain – as just one example – has become increasingly eager to develop a UAV capability far beyond that provided by the Royal Artillery's Phoenix UAV.[52]

Conclusion

As well as the undoubted benefits of UAVs in terms of their ability to spend long hours loitering above the battlefield, the political aspects of such systems are also worthy of note. As Rod Thornton observed, the 'ultimate advantage' of UAVs is that they are 'able to do the "dirty, dull and dangerous" work' which may place aircrew at risk.[53] A shot-down UAV does not carry the same political ramifications as that which would accompany a downed aircraft carrying a pilot. As Patrick Eberle notes; 'With a UAV, you do not have pilots shot down, being dragged through the streets, and globally televised.'[54] There are no casualties to account for to the public and, arguably of a far greater value strategically, no potential for captured pilots to be used as political pawns by foreign regimes.

Such hazards have been apparent since the shooting down of a U-2 over the Soviet Union in 1960 and the subsequent show trial of its pilot, Gary Powers. His capture led to the collapse of the Paris summit between the superpowers, and was a profound embarrassment to the United States. The US found itself in a similar situation with China in April 2001, as a US Navy EP-3 reconnaissance plane was hit by Chinese fighter aircraft, forcing the crew to land on the Chinese island of Hainan and inflaming tense relations between Washington and Beijing.[55] Although not discussed widely, there is evidence that the US has moved away from potentially dangerous manned overflights, and instead has opted to use UAVs on reconnaissance missions over Iran, thus immunising itself from the danger of letting its service personnel become political tools for negotiations.[56] The US has even gone as far as incorporating stealth technology into specifically designed intelligence gathering UAVs. According to "aerospace officials" the US has already used a classified Lockheed-Martin stealth UAV in operations over Iraq during the main invasion.[57] Conversely, the Iranians appear to have returned the favour, conducting UAV operations over Iraq since 2003; one UAV was shot down early in 2009 after interception by USAF F-16s.[58]

Thus, the first decade of the 21st Century has, in many ways seen the unmanned aerial vehicle take its place as an essential element of air power. Yet despite the impressive achievements of UAVs, difficulties remain. As discussed elsewhere in this book, the legal and ethical issues surrounding UAVs are an area still to be explored. The use of a Predator to kill a leading al Qaeda member in Yemen in 2002 was denounced by the Swedish foreign minister as 'a summary execution that violates human rights', while the employment of an unmanned platform to carry out this strike raised a number of concerns about 'remote killing'.[59] These concerns have not, to date, affected the use of UAVs in such operations, most notably those by the US against militants in Pakistan in support of Operation Enduring Freedom, and by the Israelis, who conducted their own UAV attacks against Hamas militants in 2005.[60]

Furthermore, UAVs, rather akin to the first military aircraft, can only provide their essential information, or attack enemy targets when the weather is reasonable. UAVs are subjected to weather limitations, which can severely affect performance. They are still relatively fragile craft, and the inevitable lack of complete situational awareness of operators has seen them suffer a high level of attrition. Also, there is debate over who should control UAVs and how they should be operated – some UAV proponents bemoan the fact that the air forces utilising this technology have insisted on the more complex systems being operated by rated pilots. Opponents of this view, however, point out that operating in airspace which is occupied (even if only temporarily) by other aircraft requires the operator to possess the same degree of comprehension as a trained pilot. Near misses between cargo aircraft and UAVs over Afghanistan and instances of combat aircraft being surprised at the presence of a UAV which was thought to be more than twenty miles away suggest that , at least for the moment, the possession of airmanship skills is necessary for those operating UAVs at any notable altitude.[61]

Nevertheless, the Israeli experiences of the early 1980s helped to illustrate the value and viability of the UAV as a tool of war. Although there had been some reluctance to follow suite in the United States – and, as a result, amongst many of its Allies – the value of the information obtained even by only a small force of unmanned platforms during Operation Desert Storm pointed the way forward. Operation Allied Force, for all the difficulties associated with that campaign, provided the springboard as military commanders began to fully appreciate the way in which UAVs could dramatically enhance their access to vital information. By the time the US and its Allies came to deploy to Afghanistan and then Iraq, there was little doubt that the UAV had arrived as a major player in modern conflict. It may still, in 2008, be an emergent technology in many ways, but UAV at last has a foothold as an essential component within modern military forces, taking air power in new directions and offering a new spectrum of capabilities to commanders at all levels. There will inevitably be hazards along the way, but the past decade has seen the UAV finally come of age.

NOTES

[1] Gunilla Herolf, 'The Future of Unmanned Aircraft', in Frank Barnanby and Marlies Ter Borg, *Emerging Technologies and Military Doctrine: A Political Assessment* (London: Macmillan, 1986), p.148. The term 'RPV' remained in widespread use throughout the 1980s and early 1990s, and is used interchangeably with the

term 'UAV' in this chapter when referring to events during this period.

[2] General Accounting Office, *DOD's use of Remotely Piloted Vehicle technology offers opportunities for saving lives and Dollars* (Washington, GAO, 1981), p.8. The GAO changed its name to the Government Accountability Office in 2004, and the old name, as the issuing authority, is used here.

[3] As a further instance of the importance of reducing casualties amongst armed forces numerically inferior to those of neighbouring Arab nations driving Israeli military planning, the development of the heavily-armoured Merkava main battle tank is instructive. Although the weight of the vehicle compromised the speed and mobility that were otherwise useful in the sort of armoured desert warfare the IDF embarked upon in 1967 and 1973, the benefits of heavy armour were deemed to offset this disadvantage.

[4] Anthony H Cordesman and Abraham R Wagner, *The Lessons of Modern War, Volume 1: The Arab Israeli Conflicts 1973-1989* (Boulder: Westview Press, 1990), p.189.

[5] Ibid, p.190.

[6] Ibid, p.191.

[7] Ibid, p. 208

[8] Ibid, p.209.

[9] Bill Sweetman, 'HALE/MALE Unmanned Air Vehicles: Part 1: History of the Endurance UAV', in *International Air Power Review*, Volume 15 (2005), p.59.

[10] Ibid, pp.60-61.

[11] U.S. Government Accounting Office, Unmanned Vehicles: Assessment of DOD's Unmanned Aerial Vehicle Master Plan,(Washington: GAO 1988), p. 6.

[12] Michael T Jordan, 'Merging the Tribes: Streamlining DoD's Acquisition of Unmanned Aerial Systems', US Army War College Strategy Research Project, 2006.
Available at http://www.dtic.mil/cgi-bin/GetTRDoc?AD=ADA449383&Location=U2&doc=GetTRDoc.pdf [accessed 20 June 2008]..

[13] Ibid, pp.64-65.

[14] The captured airman, Lieutenant Robert Goodman, is reputed to have been told by a Syrian guard: 'Jackson is coming to get you.' To this, Goodman is alleged to have sarcastically replied 'Oh yeah – which one? Reggie or Michael?' See Mark Morgan and Rick Morgan, *Intruder: The Operational History of Grumman's A-6* (Atglen: Schiffer Military History, 2004), p.163, fn.3.

[15] Major Doug Thrash, *Remotely Piloted Vehicles: The Unexploited Force* Multiplier, US Marine Corps Command and Staff College Thesis, 1989, http://www.globalsecurity.org/intell/library/reports/1989/TGD.htm.

[16] US General Accounting Office, *Unmanned Aerial Vehicles: DoD's Demonstration Approach Has Improved Project Outcomes* GAO/NSIAD-99-33 (Washington: GAO, 1993), p.2.

[17] Harlan Geer and Christopher Bolkcom, *Unmanned Aerial Vehicles: Background and Issues for Congress*, Congressional Research Service report for Congress, November 21, 2005, p.3.

[18] Anthony H Cordesman and Abraham R Wagner, *The Lessons of Modern War, Volume IV: The Gulf War* (Boulder: Westview Press, 1996), p.321.

[19] Ibid.

[20] Richard P Hallion, *Storm Over Iraq: Air Power and the Gulf War* (Washington: Smithsonian Institute, 1992), p.312. It should be noted that while the attempted surrender is not in doubt, Hallion's account slightly conflicts with others which suggest that the Pioneer was under control when the incident occurred.

[21] John L Trefz, *From Persistent ISR to Precision Strikes: The Expanding Role of UAVs* (Newport, RI: Naval War College, 2003) p.7.

[22] Cordesman and Wagner, *Lessons of Modern War, IV*, p. 320

[23] Ibid, p.323.

[24] Bill Yenne, *Attack of the Drones: A History of Unmanned Aerial Combat* (St Paul: Zenith Press, 2004), p.59.

[25] Sweetman, 'Endurance UAV part 1' (Note 9), p.67.

[26] Ibid

[27] Sweetman, *Endurance UAV Part 1* (note 9), p.70.

[28] Geer and Bolkom, *Unmanned Aerial Vehicles* (Note 17), p.11.

[29] Major General Kenneth R Israel, 'Modeling and Simulation Employed in the Predator Unmanned Aerial Vehicle Program' (Washington: Defense Airborne Reconnaissance Office, 1997) available at **http://www.fas.org/irp/agency/daro/product/predms.htm** [accessed 16 June2008].

[30] Ibid.

[31] The Rambouillet talks were held by some to have been pointless, in that the terms on offer were impossible for Milosevic to accept – see the evidence to the House of Commons Select Committee on Defence given by Lord Gilbert, Question 1086 in House of Commons Select Committee on Defence, *Lessons of Kosovo: Minutes of Evidence and Appendices* (London: TSO, 2000), in which he suggests that the Rambouillet terms were designed to be unacceptable and thus provoke a fight – Lord Gilbert was a minister in the Ministry of Defence at the time of the conflict. For a contemporary account of the Rambouillet conference, see Marc Weller, 'The Rambouillet Conference on Kosovo', *International Affairs*, Vol.75, No.2 (April 1999, pp.211-251).

[32] Tim Ripley, 'UAVs over Kosovo – did the earth move?' *Defence Systems Daily*, 1 December 1999, **http://defence-data.com/features/fpage34.htm** [accessed 21 June 2008].

[33] Benjamin S Lambeth, *NATO's Air War for Kosovo* (Santa Monica: RAND, 2001), p.95 and Director, Operational Test & Evaulation, Fiscal Year 99 Report, available at **http://www.globalsecurity.org/military/library/budget/fy1999/dot-e/airforce/99predator.html** [accessed 17 June 2008].

[34] The Phoenix experienced a number of unfortunate problems during its early development and initial operational use, not aided by its configuration which required it to invert before landing, under parachute, on an air bag which was meant to cushion the sensor group from damage. It acquired the nickname of 'the bugger off' amongst some users 'because it frequently did, never to return'. Michael Evans, *The Times* 12 August 2008, http://www.timesonline.co.uk/tol/news/politics/article4510403.ece [accessed 12 August 2008].

[35] Lambeth, *NATO's Air War*, (note 32) pp.96-97.

[36] For instance, see House of Commons Select Committee on Defence, *Fourteenth Report: Lessons of Kosovo* (London: TSO, 2000), Paragraph 127.

[37] Lambeth, *NATO's Air War*, (Note 32) p.96.

[38] Brigadier Andrew Figgures, evidence to House of Commons Select Committee on Defence, 12 April 2000, in Select Committee on Defence, *Lessons of Kosovo: Evidence* (Note 30), Question 517.

[39] The Ministry of Defence decided not to proceed with the smaller Watchkeeper 180 variant, and all the British Army's Watchkeepers will now be based on the Hermes 450. A small number of Hermes 450s are, at time of writing (2008) in use under an Urgent Operational Requirement.

[40] 'Applying UAV lessons to transform the battlefield', Speech by Secretary of the Air Force James Roche to the Association of Unmanned Vehicles Systems International, Baltimore, July 15, 2003.

[41] Ibid.

[42] Ibid.

[43] Ibid.

[44] Tim Ripley, 'UAVs over Kosovo - did the Earth move?' Defence Systems Daily, 1 December 1999 http://defence-data.com/features/fpage34.htm [Accessed 26 May 2008].

[45] Major Phil M. Haun, USAF, Air Power Versus A Fielded Army: A Construct For Air Operations In The 21st Century (Maxwell, 2001), p.19 Available at https://research.au.af.mil/papers/ay2001/acsc/01-054.pdf [accessed 22 May 2008]

[46] Bill Sweetman, 'HALE/MALE Unmanned Air Vehicles Part 2: 21st Century Warfighters', *International Air Power Review*, Volume 16, p.43.

[47] Bill Yenne, *Attack of the Drones*: p.87.

[48] David Martin, 'The Predator: The Most Valuable Weapon in the American Arsenal?', CBS News website, 7 January 2003, available at **http://www.cbsnews.com/stories/2003/01/07/60II/main535569.shtml** [accessed 28 June, 2008]; Yenne, *Attack*, p.88.

[49] Ibid.

[50] David Jordan, 'Countering Insurgency from the Air: The Postwar Lessons', *Contemporary Security Policy*, Volume 28 No.1 (2007), p.103.

[51] Sweetman, 'Unmanned Aerial Vehicles: Part 1' (Note 9), p.43.

[52] Command 6041-I *Delivering Security in a Changing World: Defence White Paper* (London: TSO, 2003), p.10 and Command 6269, *Delivering Security in a Changing World: Future Capabilities* (London: TSO, 2004).

[53] Rod Thornton, *Asymmetric Warfare; Threat and response in the 21st Century'* (Cambridge: Polity press, 2007), p.94.

[54] Capt Patrick Eberle, 'To UAV or not to UAV: That is the Question: Here is One Answer' *Air & Space Power Journal* (October 2001) , http://www.airpower.maxwell.af.mil/airchronicles/cc/eberle.html.

[55] Congressional Research Service (2001) 'China-U.S. Aircraft Collision Incident of April 2001: Assessments and Policy Implications' (The Library of Congress, 2001), p.2 - http://www.fas.org/sgp/crs/row/RL30946.pdf.

[56] Dafna Linzer, 'U.S. Uses Drones to Probe Iran for Arms' Washington Post, 13 February 2005.

[57] DA Fulchum, 'Stealth UAV goes to war' *Aviation Week & Space Technology*, Vol. 159, no. 1 (July 2003), pp. 20-21.

[58] 'Coalition Jets shoot down Iranian UAV over Iraq' American Forces Press Service, 16 March 2009, **http://www.defenselink.mil/news/newsarticle.aspx?id=53495** (accessed 19 March 2009).

[59] CBS News, *Remote Controlled Spyplanes*, 6 November 2002 at **http://www. cbsnews.com/stories/2002/11/06/attack/main528396.shtml** [accessed 17 June 2008].

[60] Aaron Klein 'Israel's secret drone revealed' (03/06/05) *World Net Daily*, **http:// www.wnd.com/news/article.asp?ARTICLE_ID=44566**

[61] Ade Orchard, with James Barrington, *Joint Force Harrier: The Inside Story of a Royal Navy Fighter Squadron at War* (London: Michael Joseph, 2008) pp.238-240.

UNMANNED AERIAL VEHICLES IN THE ROYAL
AIR FORCE - 2047

Wg Cdr Richard M. Mcmahon

'In the development of air power, one has to look forward and not backward to figure out what is going to happen'

> Brigadier General Billy Mitchell,
> Deputy Chief of the US Air
> Service, 1919-24

Introduction

The task to predict how the RAF will develop and exploit Unmanned Air Vehicles (UAV) over the next 40 or so years provides a fascinating opportunity to consider developments based upon the combination of known technological advances and those that could be possible in the future. While looking backward may go against the opening quote, it should be recognised that advances in aviation and space technology have been far greater and more rapid than any of those achieved by man on land or at sea. In the early years of aviation development, technological advances from the Wright brothers first flight[1] to the 'Supermarine' Spitfire do not appear that great.[2] However, even over this relatively short period in terms of war fighting, the man in the machine has proved a significant constraining factor on range and endurance. The effect of removing crews from the Avro Lancaster and replacing them with additional fuel and ordinance could have enabled Air Marshal 'Bomber Harris' to achieve similar effects against Nazi Germany with an aircraft fleet one third of the size.[3] With the advent of the Jet engine, the endurance constraints became less of a factor while physiological issues started to limit aerial platform development. Advances from the sub-sonic Canberra Mk1[4] to the hugely expensive and capable B2 bomber have been considerable. Platform speed, range and payloads have increased along with the accuracy of air-to-ground weapons. However, the man-in-the-loop (MIL) has remained the constant constraining factor. Equally, advances in the more agile combat aircraft from the single role English Electric Lightning[5] to the multi-role F35 Lightning II (Joint Strike Fighter[6]) while impressive, are still constrained by the requirement for a 'cockpit' and life support systems. Indeed, the agility of these modern platforms is not limited by aircraft design but by the physiological 'g' tolerance of pilots. Therefore, the prospect of designing and building unmanned combat air vehicles unfettered by human constraints is both exciting and daunting. On one hand, replacing complex life support systems with advanced communication and control systems seems entirely feasible; while on the other, dealing with the implications of removing the pilot creates an even greater challenge. In particular, there are understandable safety concerns. These come from the civilian pilot unions, military aviators and national and international regulators. Many of these concerns, while open to accusations of self-preservation, actually provide useful benchmarks for the development of UAV which must all be met.

'Predicting the future is easy, the hard part is getting it right!'

Anon

Equally daunting is the breath of this military topic and its civil dependencies. Although the civil sector of employment and development is not covered in detail, without this involvement and the desire to exploit unmanned capabilities, funding and technological resource would be scarce indeed. Fortunately, the business and service sectors have recognised the huge potential and breadth of capability afforded by UAV. Many uses are obvious such as the monitoring of lines of communication[7] , however, policing of these and other key assets could be faster and easier while also detecting and possibly preventing vandalism and other activity from unexpected threats in this uncertain world. Unlike many other air and space capabilities, the civil sector is leading the way on many areas of UAV development such as the requirement for a 'Sense & Avoid' (S&A) system that is at least as comparable in its performance with man in the cockpit.

Building upon future plans for military UAV activity in 2007 and based upon the current rate of technological development, the role for UAV in 2047 may not be so obvious or apparent. Indeed, future advances in nanotechnology may transform the way people, weapons and equipment are tracked and identified, potentially nullifying the current conventions which drive our military need for active ISR. Continuing this theme, the dependence upon space and satellites for communications and data fusion should not be overlooked. Western dominance in this environment arena cannot be assumed[8] and the need for a rapid development in autonomous unmanned systems may be critical. Currently we categorize UAV into HALE, MALE[9] , Tactical, Mini and Micro-UAV and generally, we align these categories with Strategic, Operational and Tactical roles. In line with known technological advances, it may be necessary to review these roles. There may be a similar requirement as the impact of developments in propulsion systems and Directed Energy Weapons (DEW) start to take effect. Also, while we should celebrate the collaborative UK UAV industrial efforts, we should not discount the advances made by our allies both in Europe and USA. Finally, without international regulatory approval, UAV development will be limited and constrained to combat arenas (effectively segregated airspace), we cannot afford to discount this issue. As with any emerging capability, clear and agreed terminology is vital for the understanding of discussion. While UAV refers to individual unmanned platforms, Unmanned Air Systems (UAS) is a better discriminator for discussing management of the end-to-end capability, i.e. from the control consul via the unmanned cockpit to the war fighter below.

As we look at the development of UAS, the future of manned combat aviation remains a constant underlying theme. That question is examined throughout this essay by discussion of issues such as data processing, tactical decision making and the complexity of military operations. The intent is to provide pointers to the future, based upon commonly expected advances in technology and combat operations.

Current Capability

As we look to the future, it is interesting to examine the potential impact of Moore's Law[10] upon UAV/S development. Although this empirical observation was made in 1965, the doubling of computer power has continued to this day. So far, the effect upon computer equipment and software has been seismic. If we look forward another 40 years, the 'doubling in 18 months law' would see a factor of a 32 million increase in performance/capability.[11] Of course, while it may be unrealistic to see these advances transfer in their totality to aviation technology, it is reasonable to expect significant progress in the coming years. Although this essay focuses upon RAF developments and should acknowledge that MOD resource will always be a constraining factor, the global civil sector involvement in research and development is likely to generate many solutions which could see UAV become more capable and affordable in the near future. Therefore, RAF future aspirations should not be constrained by resource and, in line with current Defence Industrial Strategy, the MOD will look to exploit every opportunity to achieve best value for money.

Examination of current operations in Iraq and Afghanistan highlights the enduring need for an ISR capability that can provide services ranging from 24/7 'pattern of life' monitoring to short-term Full Motion Video dissemination in support of specific troop actions. Between these two boundaries, there lies a broad range of ISR requirement dependant upon the mission, the environment and the threat. The longstanding catchphrase of the four 'D's' - 'Deep, Dull, Dirty and Dangerous' will continue to underpin the ISR requirement, the challenge is to identify how this will be delivered over the next 40 years. In parallel with the advances in our unmanned ISR capability, rising cost and competing demands for resource and skilled personnel will only increase the demand for the delivery of 'multi-role' unmanned capabilities. In the manned environment, the RAF has recognised this in the development of plans for Typhoon[12] and JCA. We should not forget, however, that ISTAR[13] is but one of the 6 enduring Core Air and Space Power Roles (CASPR) and while tempting to examine this activity within the environmental bounds of the FASOC, the immediate and enduring purpose of UAV ISR will continue to be the provision of timely and critical support to joint operations. The challenge is how we best manage the two potentially conflicting capabilities of enduring ISR and high value asset attack.

All future UAV enhancements will depend upon developments in the key components of the UAV family. One useful benchmark for these components can be found in the US Joint Concept of Operations for Unmanned Aircraft Systems[14] and they are categorized as follows: the unmanned aircraft, the payload[15], communications, the control element, support equipment and the human component. As with the defence lines of development, it is logical to expect appropriate attention to all the components if military forces are to fully exploit this emerging capability.

Following the defeat of Saddam Hussein's forces, UK and US stabilising forces encountered significant terrorist threats, asymmetric in nature and driven by suicidal beliefs. It was quickly recognised that our forces faced a significant capability gap in terms of ISR. Ideally, the coalition would like the ability to monitor patterns of life, 24/7 across all of Iraq. However, resource in terms of platforms and the ability to analyse such a huge quantity of data currently make such an option both impracticable and unaffordable. Part of the UK response came in Mar 04 with the formation of a USAF/RAF Combined Joint Predator Task Force (CJPTF) to support land operations in key areas of Iraq. Originally based at Nellis AFB and operating the MQ-1 Predator A UAV[16] , the unit has enjoyed considerable operational success while also contributing significantly to USAF and RAF decisions to acquire the larger and far more capable successor to Predator, the MQ-9 Reaper.

UK Reaper

When compared with Predator A, the Reaper represents a major evolution of the UAV. It is four times heavier, at a gross weight of five tons and is similar in size to the USAF A-10 Thunderbolt II aircraft. The plane can carry many more weapons than the Predator A, having the ability to carry 14 AGM-114 Hellfire II anti-armour missiles, or four Hellfire and two 500 pound bombs. The MQ-9 Reaper is also designed to deploy precision guided weapons such as the GBU-12 and the 500lb GBU-38 JDAM.[17] Operational cruise will be at around 260 kts while the platform will avoid 'MANPADS'[18] and small-arms threats by operating at around altitudes of 25000 ft for sortie durations of up to 18 hours. Key to the capability is the onboard sensor suite. In parallel with the USAF, the RAF has opted to employ the MTS-B Sensor Ball and Lynx SAR/GMTI. This will incorporate imaging sensors to provide video and still-frame, Electro-Optical (EO), infrared and Synthetic Aperture Radar (SAR) radar, infrared, laser and radar targeting.

In general terms, the tasking for Reaper will follow normal coalition activities within a standard NATO planning cycle. As with all air platforms, Reaper will be tasked through the Air Tasking Order (ATO) and crews will work with both Joint Force and Air Component assets to co-ordinate effort and the best delivery of effect. Once tasked, the Launch and Recovery Element (LRE) oversee the preparation, launch, recovery, refuelling, rearming and maintenance of the Reaper from its secure forward operating base. After take-off and normally while within LOS of the LRE, the Reaper is 'handed-off' to the Mission crew (pilot & sensor operator[19]) via satellite communications. Although this may seem hazardous, high levels of communications redundancy and auto flight control systems minimize the risk during this process. As with any other air platform, the Mission crew have access to a normal suite of communications which allows them to coordinate their sortie with other key Air C2 elements such as airborne platforms like the E3 AWACS or with ground units through forward air controllers or coalition equivalents. Indeed, by having a full ATC service, the Reaper can 'roam' an AOR with high levels of safety and with the capacity to take avoiding action against other friendly or hostile conflicting air traffic. This roaming ability provides the Joint Force Commander (JFC) with additional operational flexibility and the opportunity to respond to developing threats outside the original planning AOR.

It is important, however, to recognise that the rapid rate of UAV evolution, presents both operators and commanders with a growing and complex challenge. In its earliest form, the Phoenix UAV was employed primarily as an organic ISR platform and due to its short range and endurance, it did not figure in the ATO. However, with emerging tactical platforms operating at ranges in excess of 50km from control stations, at altitudes over 5000 ft and with an on-task time of over 5 hours, mission planners must take careful account of tactical UAV operations. Equally, owners of these organic capabilities will need to integrate their systems into the broader ATO process, potentially exposing their capability to the demands of other coalition partners.

In contrast, strategic/operational UAV that possess an ability to roam while fitted with kinetic weapons, demand that the planners balance the requirements for ISR tasking with capabilities to provide direct effects in support of Land operations such as 'Troops in Contact' (TIC). With an ability to combine all functions of the targeting cycle, F2E2EA[20] , command of such a capability presents a mouth-watering challenge. While tempting to suggest that a TIC scenario should always have a higher priority, other factors must be taken into consideration. Platform response, other FJ or AH CAS options or, most telling, competing strategic ISR requirements[21] are certain to complicate the decision process. Equally, as UAV become faster, can carry more weapons and remain on task for longer, the complexity of this problem increases. Therefore, concept documents covering the operations, employment and use of platforms will be vital. Integration into Joint Operations will be a key issue, while the authors must also take account of differing and emerging UAV employment policies and identify the best fit for the UK military model.[22] Furthermore, continually evolving platform and attack capabilities will demand that these documents are updated on a regular basis.

Once on station, careful management of the broad array of sensors is essential if the Reaper platform is to deliver its full potential and provide operational and tactical commanders with high quality data resolution combined with a range of perspectives suitable for exploitation, analysis and possibly targeting.[23] Outputs must be available to the full range of tactical actors to improve the realisation of Effects.[24] At times, the delivery of Full Motion Video in support of TIC will be the priority task. However, given the paucity of ISR assets, operational control of Reaper will be a significant command challenge, particularly when the platform is armed. Equally, ground forces must understand the capability, appreciate its significant advantages in terms of combining 'sensor & shooter' while also accepting the limitations in terms of weapons payload and platform speed. In short, Reaper should be seen as one part of the air capability and not, quite simply, as the only all encompassing solution.

With Mission crews based in the US, they face a number of challenges. The most immediate is the perception from those under direct hostile fire that supporting rear-elements such as 39 Squadron Reaper crews are unaffected by the threats and dangers of operations.[25] Of course, once the platform has demonstrated its capability, by identifying emerging threats, by delivering its own weapons or by providing laser designation for a weapons drop from a coalition fighter in support of TIC, the attitude will change. However, the challenge for these crews will not change. While personnel operating Reaper are in constant support of combat operations, they face a recurring education challenge as troop roulements occur. The benefits of sustained crewing of Reaper are tangible. Levels of expertise, familiarity with the environment, the terrain, the threat and operational procedures remain at a constant high. Predator/Reaper Mission Crews are probably the best qualified to contribute to mission planning while also fully exploiting the UAV capability. Similar benefits accrue from the dissemination of data to home-based Image Analysts (IA) where they can profit from the application of highly advanced and sensitive software tools to carry out detailed analysis and targeting. One of the additional benefits of this 'Reachback' is that data can be shared and exploited to meet differing demands and then stored for future reference in support of later operations. As ever, bandwidth, exploitation facilities and available expertise may limit how, where and when such data can be treated and disseminated.

The RAF's acquisition of Reaper has followed the UOR[26] process commencing with a submission in Jul 06. As Reaper is a US capability, the purchase was complicated by laws covering Foreign Military Sales (FMS) which involves an approvals process requiring Congressional review. Given that the first platform deployed to Afghanistan in October 07 – the 15-month period between defining the requirement to the delivery of an operational capability demonstrates a remarkable level of both international and inter-departmental cooperation and effort to achieve this success. Benefiting from the considerable experienced gained from CJPTF ops, the organisation, training, personnel and infrastructure DLODs, while challenging to resolve, have been relatively straight forward to address. As ever, UK Defence Equipment & Sustainment (DE&S) staffs have relished the tight timelines, although 'normal' best practice for equipment programmes has, at times, contrived to protract the UOR process. In sum, the delivery of a fully weaponized UAV capability to the RAF in less than 18 months has been an outstanding achievement which may yet set new standards and challenges for our defence acquisition organisations.

Future Capability - Near-term

Moving away from a US 'Commercial off the Shelf' (COTS) solution, UK industries in partnership with the MOD are working on a number of other

UAV capability developments. For example, BAE Systems are currently experimenting with a small UAV known as High Intensity Rapid Technology Insertion (HERTI). In collaboration with the Air Warfare Centre, the platform has been deployed to Afghanistan under the guise of Project Morrigan. The aim is to investigate and evaluate the limitations and potential of an autonomous UAV in the Joint Battlespace. Additional objectives and tasks should contribute to the force protection and safety of our ground forces. This ambitious private venture project gives a clear indication of the high level of interest from UK industry in delivering added value to basic UAV ISR capabilities. Levels of autonomy enhanced by on-board data processing and mission management will be vital to help avoid an over dependence on lines of communication and should allow operators to exploit the full potential of the UAV. Indeed, as we look to the future, resource constraints are certain to limit the number of UAV systems in use with the MOD preferring, no doubt, to build upon the capabilities of emerging fleets. Therefore, assuming the lack of a more affordable alternative, platforms such as the Reaper and Watchkeeper, could, like many other venerable ISR platforms[27] , be expected to withstand the test of time and deliver effect for a minimum period of 25 years. The challenge within this essay is to identify a capability which falls outside the planning for High Level Operational Concepts(HLOC) – as pointed out in the HLOC,[28]

> 'No reliable methodology or technology has been developed that can ensure accurate predictions about the future'

Despite that alibi, there are some good indications of how UAV will be developed in the future. BAE Systems in concert with MoD's Strategic Unmanned Air Vehicle (Experiment) (SUAV(E)) IPT, are exploring and demonstrating how emerging technologies and systems can deliver battle-winning capabilities for the UK armed forces. They are the prime contractor and industry lead for the development of 'TARANIS' which will be the largest UAV yet built in the UK. Included in the consortium are other leading UAV exponents in the guise of QinetiQ, Rolls-Royce and Smiths Aerospace. The following BAE press release provides a clear indicator of the state of UAV autonomy today:

> "The brains of TARANIS are now designed and coherent and the system can autonomously control the aircraft to taxi, take off, and navigate its way to a search area while reacting to any threats or other events. It will then route its way around the search area in whichever way it wants to, locate the target, and then use its sensor system to transmit a series of images and views back to the operator to confirm it is the target to be attacked. Then, once it has been authorized to do so, it autonomously attacks that target, routes its way back home, lands and taxies back.'

Subsequent comment also focused on the targeting and attack capability rather than the surveillance and reconnaissance roles. Given that flight trials are due to commence in 2010, the prospects for building a completely autonomous UAV by 2047 seem assured. Confirming the pedigree of the UK's UAV exponents, QinetiQ have recently enjoyed demonstrable success with their recent[29] unofficial world endurance record for the Zephyr UAV. Powered by the sun and solar batteries, the platform, which weighs less than 32 Kgs and can carry and operate lightweight digital ISR systems. Zephyr flew for over 82 hours at altitudes in excess of 55000 ft, before achieving a safe landing at the US military Yuma Proving Grounds in Arizona. Of note was that the aircraft used its solar electrical power system through three complete diurnal cycles – another good indicator of what should be possible in 40 years.[30] Whether such a system is used as an alternative for satellite systems or as an emergency fall-back option will depend upon cost and the growing threat to space satellite operations. A vital requirement that allows operators to exploit this extended capability will be autonomy. In this arena, QinetiQ engineers recently publicised an emerging capability by demonstrating the ability to operate and control four UAV from the backseat of a Tornado F3 under Project TIARA.[31] Underpinning these individual company initiatives, UK companies are collaborating under the ASTRAEA[32] banner to work with non-military UK government departments to fund specific research into UAV. Amounting to a £32m investment over 3 years, companies are working with academia on 16 issues covering UAV Technology, Regulation and Demonstration. These subjects, which will be crucial to future UAV development, include communications, collision avoidance and propulsion. Furthermore, the output should underpin much of the ongoing work to develop platforms such as TERRANIS, HERTI, UK Reaper, H450 and its planned successor Watchkeeper.[32]

Other exploratory UAV activity includes the UK Army investigations into Loitering Munitions. Where such a system would fit into the Joint Battle space and how it could be safely exploited and integrated needs careful examination. Key issues such as airspace control, Sense & Avoid, C2, ROE and 'ownership-of-the-bomb' will not be easy to resolve with competing Service doctrines demanding different conclusions. Furthermore, while it may seem possible to allow such a system a high level of autonomy another considerable challenge will be the development of systems and TTPs that ensure effective direct support to Land operations in a non-permissive air environment. Air Defence of a routinely static system which has a roving capability would be extremely complex. However, the benefits of this system could bring into question the long-term future of the traditional artillery battery. With troop commanders potentially having the ability to call upon a buffet of airborne weapons effects they may wish to see resource spent on more of these platforms rather than on force protection, logistics and sustainment for artillery units. Finally, while issues such as 'platform ownership' and executive authority may appear as 'soft issues', they could present a challenge which is far more complex than any technical issue, particularly in a collation environment.

On the international stage, interest in UAV continues apace. In terms of expenditure, the USA lead the way with billions of dollars earmarked for UAV development in support of Homeland Defence and the GWOT.[34] However, while much of this funding is focused upon organic equipment programmes, US military and civil contractors are working closely with NATO and European allies to develop standards and protocols to enable international UAV operations. Even at this early stage of UAV evolution, there is clear international agreement on the potential and need for civil unmanned systems. Initially, roles will focus on government activities ranging from traffic surveillance to counter terrorism within national borders. As confidence in UAV grows, other national civilian/industrial developments will follow. Although the airline pilots associations can identify credible and reasonable objections to unpiloted airline fleets, these merely present useful and additional safety hurdles which engineers and scientists are sure to overcome. The real challenge will be cultural and there is certain to be a need for a transitional 'safety-pilot' period to help overcome these natural concerns.[35] However, once unmanned aviation has a demonstrable safety record, the acceptance and commercial demand for unmanned systems will certainly grow. Within Europe, there is recognition that collaboration is the only answer to delivering a pan-European solution to challenges such as 'Sense & Avoid'. Indeed, this form of collaboration should help to convince regulators such as Eurocontrol to accept the minimum safety requirement identified by a coalition of national contributors. Although focusing upon Europe, a regulatory environment which recognises the international dimension of airspace use and the pivotal role of ICAO should be self-evident. It is in this global arena that military UAV operations will get very difficult. However, while not wishing to underestimate the complexity of national UAV activity and approvals, once civil UAV start to cross national borders regulatory agreement in some areas such as frequency spectrum appear as a far off nirvana. For example, such a proposition requires agreement upon access to a local R/F spectrum which does not generate conflicts with other operators like the ambulance service or mobile phone network. International progress in this area will require extra-ordinary levels of agreement at the World Radio Conference which meets only every 4 years.[36] In civil aviation, a solution to frequency spectrum issues should be found. However, if we then add the very significant complication of a UAV proponent employing military UAV (ISR or armed), international agreement or cooperation is more difficult and alternative methods of C2 will be required.

From a national and European perspective, we should be aware of other softer concerns raised by organisations such as Liberty. Concerns regarding the 'Big Brother' culture will only increase and development in UAS will have to take account of national laws covering 'Freedom of Information' and 'Human Rights'. How is the data stored? Who has access to it? How is information exploited? These are all examples of the questions that will arise. While not attempting to address these issues, they give a useful indicator of the legislative challenges associated with the general acceptance of military UAV operations.

Future Capability - Medium Term

Following the early struggles over the next 10 to 15 years, the civil airline industry could be at the forefront of regular commercial UAV flights. Freight carrying airliners following minimum risk routes over the sea and avoiding areas of dense population could allow operators to reduce costs and improve efficiency while generating public confidence. Thereafter, national operators may chose to provide services within their borders before exploring European and other suitably equipped and controlled airspace. The period between 2020 and 2030 could see a major transformation in the AT industry. Indeed, one wonders why this progress has not been made with other forms of transport such as the railways – it may be that the cost of training and retaining train drivers appears insignificant when set alongside the initial investment costs required to automate an entire rail network. The same cannot be said for the cost of employing and training airline pilots. A safe and successful commercial unmanned airline operation will depend upon a mature and proven flight management system that is fully integrated into both the aircraft and ground control systems. With such a system, we could also expect to see the gradual automation of air traffic control systems. Again, the major hurdle will not be technology; rather it will be the requirement for international agreement on standards. With it, there will have to be certain mandatory regulatory requirements for all airborne systems.[37] Thereafter, it could be that the most probably risk to an unmanned commercial aircraft will come from a bird strike. So by 2025, we could be on the verge of unmanned airline transport systems. The introduction of the system will need a spiral development strategy starting for example with freight transport and then followed by commercial operators employing pilots merely to monitor aircraft systems. After such a proving period, only then will unmanned airline transport systems gain public acceptance. On the military side, things may not be so simple.

Global agreement or acceptance for military UAV operations appears a less likely outcome. What country fearing a threat from a military neighbour or super power is going to make airspace and RF spectrum available to a potential aggressor? Without secure communications, military UAV ops will be constrained. However, assuming continued Western domination in space, factors such as platform antennae position, frequency encryption and low probability of detection techniques could overcome such resistance. Given the pace of technological advance, only the most powerful nations could combat such technology.[38] However, the MIL, whether in a ground control station or an airborne platform will remain critical to all offensive operations. The laws of armed conflict (LOAC) set particularly high standards for war fighting and as with soldiers and sailors, aircrews have to pay due regard to factors such as necessity, proportionality, discrimination (collateral damage) and humanity. Therefore, it is not possible to accredit a completely autonomous UAV without acknowledging both the complexities and fluidity of sustained combat operations.[39] An autonomous system may be able to discriminate between a hostile APC and one that marked with a red cross and moving casualties. However, until a UAV possesses sensors with peripheral vision and runs on-board computer programs that have the capacity and 'intelligence' to make informed judgements regarding wide area collateral damage estimates (CDE)[40];

a totally autonomous unmanned combat air vehicle (UCAV) is unlikely to be employed in the medium term.

As one part of medium term planning, Reaper is likely to play a key part in the EC DTA[41] assessment of how they deliver DPOC.[42] Challenges will be those that face the operation and employment of all unmanned platforms but further complicated by the fitting of weapons. Static strategic targets should present no more complex problems than those for a cruise missile launch. However, UCAV attacks on mobile or transient high value targets, generate positive identity (PID) requirements which, when combined with ROE and collateral damage concerns, make C3 bandwidth an essential pre-requisite. Accepting the continuing need for MIL in the medium term, front-line UK force structures are unlikely to see significant change. For the RAF, it is likely that the Reaper force will be based in the UK supporting operational tasks while also contributing both to homeland defence and collective Trg on exercises involving Maritime ops, Land CT and Joint Air exercises such as Neptune Warrior. The Sqn is likely to be collocated with other ISR assets while LRE[43] and maintenance personnel will be deployed to support operational theatres. In parallel, No 32 Regt RA will have welcomed the introduction of Watchkeeper. During this interim period, plug-and-play capabilities and spiral development opportunities could, subject to resource, see these UAV broaden their range of activities. Much of this work will also contribute to the development of more advanced UAV systems. However, with the growth in data capture, support activities from personnel such as image analysts will increase in importance. During this interim period, the transmission, dissemination, exploitation, cataloguing, storage, and classification of data will generate a major challenge. Nothing is more compelling than the live video feed of an on-going operation. Known within the ISR community as 'Predator porn' or 'CAOC Crack' the challenge will be to ensure that the right information is disseminated to the right person at the right time. Strategic and operational commanders will have to resist the opportunity to micro-manage particular engagements, no matter how compelling the picture, rarely will they have the full tactical situation and put bluntly, such activity is not their job. Equally, effective management of imagery will be critical so that stored data is fully exploited thus ensuring the efficient use of what will continue to be a limited ISR resource.[44]

Although much of the early UAV operations will focus on ISR, offensive capabilities are certain to grow with technological advance. In particular, the small diameter bomb (SDB) will be a standard fit for UCAVs. The USAF is developing 2 variants. One version (GBU-39) is equipped with a GPS-aided inertial navigation system which makes it ideal for fixed/stationary targets such as fuel depots and bunkers while the second variant (GBU-40), includes a thermal seeker with automatic target recognition features which makes it ideal for striking fleeting targets such as tanks and mobile command posts. These are weapons openly discussed in the public domain. Therefore, it seems reasonable to speculate about weapon systems that could be in common use in 20 years. Directed Energy Weapons (DEW) currently require considerable levels of power, if this challenge can be overcome, they are certain to figure in future UCAV developments. Once these weapons prove their effectiveness, an enduring air combat presence could be sustained in permissive airspace. One interim option between UCAV employment of kinetic weapons and DEW could be the deployment of micro-UAVs launched from a UAV as a weapon. Fitted with local data links and loaded with computer algorithms, such a system could support vital 'swarm-like' search and destroy functions while also providing immediate Battle Damage Assessments.

Assuming that the UAV employs a standard propulsion system, the development of AAR will be another important challenge. Currently, Reaper can fly for over 18 hours without refuel; based upon potential advances with propulsion systems it should be possible to extend sortie times considerably. However, as ever with spiral development, as one part of a capability improves so other users of the platform look to exploit this situation. Therefore, while engine efficiency may improve, other adoptions of technological advances may combine to limit the expected increase in platform endurance. Therefore, planners should expect UAV to sustain routine ISTAR ops for 24 hours before requiring a refuel.

Current planning for UAV describes a profile of forward deployment to maximise loiter time in the AOR. While this does save transit times, UAV platforms remain vulnerable while on the ground and attract their own force protection burden. Furthermore, operating from fixed locations can limit response times while also providing advance warnings of coalition activity. Therefore, it may be necessary to find other ways to deploy UAV. It is likely that we will see the development of disposable or recyclable mini and micro-UAV. Delivered to the AOR by either other UAV or conventional air platforms, these systems could provide simple and affordable platforms to complete specific tasks ranging from the strategic to tactical in effectc.[45] Some of these systems may be pre-programmed against specific targets while others may hide and 'hibernate'[46] awaiting activation and specific ISR or targeting instructions. Such systems could make a significant contribution to intelligence service activities; it will also become necessary to have protocols to counter such systems. Some of these operations could have a significant political risk and impact, therefore, ownership in terms of operational control and employment will be an additional strategic challenge. While these platforms may appear affordable for some countries, the potential requirement for a complex C2 architecture may make there routine use impractical. Conversely, autonomous systems tasked with simple ISR activity could exploit local internet or telecom systems to relay information. Here again, advances in cyber warfare technology will be critical and could help overcome the dependencies on satellite systems and technology.

In line with these advances, we should not overlook the many ways that supported forces may exploit these systems. Given a secure communications architecture that is similar to the US Global Information Grid (GIG)[47], it should be possible to equip the foot soldier with a facility to plug into an

UAS to demand some form of immediate kinetic effect. How different is this from calling for artillery support against a specific target? This supposition generates some significant command and control issues. Currently, weapons release responsibility against ground targets sits exclusively with the aircraft commander, whether he is in the cockpit or sitting at a console. Once a soldier takes ownership of the bomb, responsibility for collateral damage becomes a contentious issue. Does it lie with the soldier or the aircraft commander? While this may appear straight-forward, the issue is further complicated if we allow a soldier to 'direct' an attack from a UCAV while under fire from hostile forces without any other C2 interaction. As with the use of artillery, it should be possible to develop overarching CONOPS and TTP[48] to address this issue, however, the work is certain to identify significant C2 issues. For example, as NATO staffs examine the concept of employment for armed UAV, the issue of weaponization generates its own discreet problems. Weapon integration, safety and operating system security are key issues for the MIL. Once you transfer that capability to the 'man-in-the-field', you complicate the original challenges while also potentially increasing the exposure of the UAS to cyber-attack from opponents in an effort to 'deny' the platforms capability.

Away from the conventional ISR and attack role, the development of UAS could see the RAF exploring other unmanned capabilities. Currently, all air platforms are manned with highly trained and experienced flight deck crews. In line with civil operations, it may be possible to configure some of our aircraft for unmanned operations, particularly for operations in permissive airspace. For example, by exploiting spiral technological advances, stand-off systems such as E3D and ASTOR could exploit emerging C3 technology so allowing both the flight deck and a number of mission crew to remain on the ground or at their home base. As confidence grows in communication networks the natural next step will be to replace the entire crew with additional systems and an automated FCS. That said, the unquantifiable capacities of the human brain (including instinct or gut feeling) are never likely to be replicated by computer technology, therefore, an onboard/on-scene Mission Commander (MC) will remain essential. However, we should recognise that utilisation of one of these platforms for trials could provide an ideal testing ground for UAV technologies such as Sense & Avoid and autonomous flight management systems. Once proven, these technologies should easily transfer both to other military platforms and civil systems. The RAF aircraft most likely to contribute to these developments are the Airbus Industries A330-200 Future Strategic Tanker Aircraft (FSTA) and A400M Tactical Transport. With their modern FCS, it should be relatively straight forward to integrate S&A hardware along with various software enhancements to allow unmanned strategic AAR & AT air operations. As part of that process, autonomous AAR to supply other UAV should be possible day or night with the option of all ac operating 'lights-out'. However, the Tactical missions are likely to be more complex with threats from small-arms fire and MANPADS affecting mission profiles. Also, certain A400M missions that demand tactical arrivals at austere airfields with damaged runways and changing ground threats will undoubtedly exceed the capabilities offered by early autonomous platforms. Given that most large ac missions will not be exposed to such threats, the number of aircrew within the 'specialist manned core' could be small. On a more positive note, it should be reasonable to expect strategic AAR platforms such as FSTA to support routine operations automatically with only occasional tactical inputs from CAOC staffs. Finally, while the modern C130J flight control systems could accommodate automatic mission management, the variety and complexity of task, could make such an option both unaffordable and impracticable.

In line with C130J operations, the conversion of our current fleet of rotary aircraft also appears unlikely. While the technology is likely to be available, cost, a requirement for detailed mission management and the needs for op agility and flexibility, will make such proposals unattractive. However, as platforms such as the Puma and the Chinook Mk2 reach the end of their service life it is likely that their replacements will operate with higher levels of automation. One major challenge will be to construct a force mix of Heavy and Tac-lift platforms that can allow pilots to manage the most complex missions. A cursory examination of helicopter operations in Afghanistan suggests that autonomous night-time 'low-level' rotary ops for logistics support, could be a viable option. Equally, in the area of SAR, a rotary system that can sustain long endurance missions at night in dangerous weather conditions could be viable. However, while it should be possible to replicate the highest levels of pilot aircraft handling skills, simple examination of the military/civil SAR and Coastguard role confirms that any operation is rarely routine and that an onboard MC supporting a winch-man/paramedic will be a pre-requisite for success.

Finally, it is necessary to complete a review of medium term developments by examining the impact that unmanned systems will have on the fighter/attack capability. Within this group we could expect to see developments affect the last years of the Apache Attack Helicopter, Typhoon and JCA. Given the complexity of attack missions, the role of the MC is certain to remain. Although advanced communication networks could ensure robust C3 links to the platforms, mission success will still depend upon traits such as ingenuity, imagination and flexibility, to name but three. In the medium term, while it should be reasonable to expect computer technology to achieve simple levels of artificial intelligence, factors such as secure communications, peripheral vision, 'on-scene' analytical skills and the Laws of Armed Conflict will continue to dictate the need for an 'on-board' brain. As with rotary operations, piloting tasks are certain to be left to computers with the man in the cockpit focusing on specific mission related and emerging tactical issues. Accepting this premise, the man-machine interface between the 'pilot-less' platforms and the MC will be vital, as will the controlled presentation of only mission essential information. Emerging improvements in Ground Control Stations are certain to contribute to these developments, as will the development of simulations to train, test and rehearse the MC. Given both the complexity of the tasks and the increased breadth of responsibility[49] , MC will need to be high calibre officers who understand fully, the aims of their mission and the array of system capabilities under their control. The MC's most often and demanding challenge will probably come from his own or other unmanned platforms seeking approval to attack or engage. In theory, advances in weapons technology, should ensure that issues such as CDE and CEP[50] will be less challenging while understanding of Cdr's Intent, ROE and LOAC will have to be exemplary. No doubt, however, 'reach-back' communications should ensure that many of the more difficult strategic/operational decisions will rest with air staffs in the CAOC.[51] Having focused on ground attack capabilities and associated efforts to operate in difficult terrain while bringing force/s to bear against targets that are relatively static, the final piece of the jig-saw comes with addressing the challenge of unmanned fighters to support Offensive and Defensive Counter Air (OCA/DCA) operations. It seems attractive to suggest that in line with complex ground attack missions, all AD fighter ops could be supported by unmanned systems. In many routine AD policing missions such an approach seems reasonable, particularly if the target platform is also unmanned. However, it is reasonable to accept that, as with SAR missions, the term 'routine' rarely applies to AD ops. While the domestic part of (10%[52]) of sorties could be executed by an unmanned system, experience suggests that the operational part (90%) of the sortie is far more complex, requiring judgemental activity, ROE decisions, visual ID and often close escort both to provide direction and to demonstrate intent. Most of these sorties will involve escorting and monitoring aircraft ranging from potential hostile bomber/ISR platforms to general air traffic such as light aircraft. In almost all these situations, a man in the cockpit will be critical to the safe outcome of an intercept. There is also the issue of public acceptance, for example, the extreme prospect of an unmanned fighter shooting down an unmanned passenger carrying commercial aircraft would generate equally extreme public reactions. That said, whether that cockpit incumbent will require the piloting skills of our current stock of fighter pilots will, as ever, be dependent upon advances in technology. Advocates of the unmanned fighter also need to appreciate that off-board decision making would require high levels of fidelity and control response that currently cannot match the performance and response levels of the human brain. Furthermore, successful unmanned combat operations against airborne targets closing at supersonic speeds depend upon constant, robust and secure communications to succeed. Although pure piloting skills are likely to become less and less relevant, as with all other air platforms requiring rapid tactical decisions, the unmanned fighter appears a long way off.

Future Capability - Long Term

Having identified the challenges facing UAS in the short and medium term, it is reasonable to expect that emerging technology will eventually provide all the solutions. However, the status quo in terms of military capability rarely exists and we should recognise that asymmetric threats to UAS C3 architecture and parallel advances in opposing technology could threaten all future UAV operations. Equally, by 2047, other space-based ISR systems and weapons could render the UAS, and even airpower in its current form, obsolete. Indeed, examination of the other environments suggests that autonomous system technology could deliver unmanned land and naval platforms thus changing the global perspective and understanding of conventional war. In addition to the conventional war-fighting environments, mobile integrated space platforms protected both by advanced protective and defensive systems including DEW are certain to transform domination of the entire battlespace. In parallel with these advances, it seems reasonable to expect that the exploitation of nanotechnology will change the way the Joint Recognised Picture is generated. The challenge lies with data gathering and tracking such that terra-bytes of information can be assimilated and fully exploited in a covert but strategic way. Exploitation of internet-technology and support systems (Cyber-warfare) could make it possible to exploit opponent communications networks such that passive data gathering becomes the norm. Detecting such activity could be very difficult with the only indication being an opponent's reduction in conventional ISR activity – by then; of course, the damage may have been done.

Mindful of constraints such as the Laws of Armed Conflict, advances in war-fighting technology may generate demands for review – however unpopular. With autonomous air vehicles potentially at the forefront of operations, the spread of technology is certain to impact upon Maritime and Land operations. For example, today the complex power source within a nuclear submarine demands constant care and attention – will this be the case in 40 years? If not, 'wither' at least half a submarine's company? Suggestions that a man is required to fire nuclear missiles fits well with the Air environment requirement for a MC. However, that is but one role. In the submarine, the many and varied 'piloting' and engineering skills could all be subsumed by an autonomous system exploiting advanced underwater S&A systems – arise the autonomous underwater vehicle (AUV). Further, ISR operations in littoral or shallow waters could be further delegated by deployable mini-AUVs. On the surface, the conventional RN 'bridge', could become redundant with crews safely accommodated in the bowels of the ship focusing on mission related activities under the command of the MC. Finally, what of the Land environment? Is it some science fiction dream to suggest that technology will deliver a combat robot, again, under the command of well equipped, data-fused combat MC? The US Army and Marine Corps have just[53] issued an urgent operational needs statement for 1000 bomb-detecting robots with a plan to have over 3000 systems in use in 5 years. While not providing an autonomous system, the levels of automation provide early indicators of what could be achieved in 25 years. Similarly, US Army plans to acquire remotely operated Unmanned Ground Vehicles (UGV) equipped with automatic weapons such as the M16 rifle, 40 mm grenade launchers and anti-tank rocket systems, reinforce this view. While there will continue to be a MIL, his location or presence will depend entirely upon the threat, the geographic environment, the level of risk and, ultimately, the complexity of the mission. A factor that will probably apply to the planning for all unmanned maritime, land and air missions in the future.

Finally, although not a specific topic of discussion, simulation will play a key part in these developments. A Mission Training Distributed Systems (MTDS) framework is certain to inform the future planning and force structures for the UAV force. Further, mission rehearsal, ATO testing, airspace integration and safety are also certain to benefit. It will also be in this arena that autonomous system T&E may occur.

Conclusion

Unbounded by current concepts and convention, and admittedly influenced by science fiction, the prospects for the employment and exploitation of unmanned air system capabilities appear unlimited. NATO countries have been quick to recognise the benefits of UAV and European industries have been working hard to match the US lead in this area. Current indicators suggest that while military requirements are driving the need for UAV development, long-term financial success will be found in the commercial arena. In the interim, developments in military capability when combined with support from accredited T&E organisations may generate a need to review air force structures. Where will the MC fit into this construct? How do we justify a MIL?

We should not underestimate other issues. Although technology is certain to advance UAV capabilities, other constraints such as resource and frequency bandwidth are certain to slow the rate of progress. In addition, opposing force capabilities will not stagnate; they will take advantage of our advances, identify vulnerabilities and pursue similar technologies to support asymmetric attacks. Our dependence on communication systems and nodes will grow and how we respond to breakdowns or attacks will be critical to operational effectiveness. These architectural factors, when combined with statutory issues such as the LOAC and the complexity of war-fighting are sure to sustain the need for MIL. In particular, our early quick wins based upon Reaper and Watchkeeper could be negated by political and military demands for greater flexibility, accuracy and responsiveness in an increasingly complex battlespace. Stealthy UAV will require direction; swarming attack systems will require mission command, long-endurance ISR platforms will require monitoring while data capture will require detailed assimilation and exploitation. Tactical attack missions will need MC to respond to unforeseen situations and changes across the war fighting environments. Unmanned commercial or military AT & AAR systems will always require some form of human interaction. While fully automatic systems should be capable of supporting routine operations, in almost all cases, manual input at some stage will be essential. The challenge will be to decide where to place that man – how do we exploit his capacity, how do we avoid overloading him and how do we empower him? Ultimately, with assured communications, total local environmental sensor coverage and complete sensor fusion, UK military unmanned air operations could, in theory, be run from PJHQ, front line commands or, on occasions, by the soldier on the ground. Delivery of such a concept that has so many uncertainties and dependencies is likely to be unaffordable, unacceptable and unachievable over any term. While technological advances may allow coalitions to shape the battlespace, individual actors and threats such as those currently in Iraq and Afghanistan may find asymmetric tools to deliver strategic counters. The ingenuity of vengeful war fighters knows no bounds; while norms may be countered, actions outside the expected will still require human interaction and command. Although the days of the 'seat-of-the-pants' aviator maybe numbered, the man in the military air vehicle, in almost every form, has a long and vital future.

NOTES

[1] 17 Dec 1903.

[2] The first flight took place 5 Mar 1936 and the aircraft flew in RAF Service until 9 Jun 57.

[3] This proposition ignores the requirement for modern avionics.

[4] First flight 13 May 1949.

[5] Introduced to Service by the RAF in Dec 1959.

[6] Known in the UK as the Joint Combat Aircraft (JCA).

[7] Road, Rail, Gas and Electricity lines, Communication Towers.

[8] China's anti-satellite missile test on 11 Jan 2007 not only demonstrated an ability to destroy space platforms from earth but the destruction produced a huge trail of identifiable debris (1335 pieces) which could still either damage or impact other low-earth space sensors.

[9] HALE – High Altitude Long Environment, MALE – Medium Altitude Long Environment.

[10] Moore's Law : 'The most popular formulation is of the doubling of the number of transistors on integrated circuits every 18 months. It is also common to cite Moore's Law to refer to the rapidly continuing advance in computing power per unit cost, because increase in transistor count is also a rough measure of computer processing power. On this basis, the power of computers per unit cost - or more colloquially, "bangs per buck" - doubles every 24 months (or, equivalently, increases 32-fold in 10 years).

[11] A more conservative interpretation of a doubling every 2 years would see this increase at a mere factor of 1 million.

[12] Original plans for Typhoon involved the formation of 7 RAF Sqns with 4 tasked with Air Defence (AD), 2 with Ground Attack (GA) and 2 with a Multi-role mission (AD/GA). Operations in Iraq and Afghanistan have reinforced the need for a multi-role capability – all RAF Typhoon Sqns will train as Multi-role.

[13] Air power's contribution to: the coordinated acquisition, processing and dissemination of timely, accurate, relevant and assured information and intelligence which supports the planning and conduct of operations, targeting and the integration of effects and enables commanders to achieve their goal throughout the Spectrum of Conflict. – JWP 0-01.1.

[14] Published Mar 07.

[15] The payload is broken down into: Sensors, Communications Relay, Weapons, Cargo and Payload Support.

[16] It is reasonable to consider the Predator A as the first, long-range BLOS Unmanned Combat Air Vehicle – it entered service in 1995.

[17] Joint Direct Attack Munition with a stand-off capability of around 15 nm

[18] Man Portable Air Defence Systems such Stinger IR Missiles.

[19] On most sorties the crew will be joined by an Intelligence Analyst to assist with imagery exploitation.

[20] Find, fix, track, target, engage, assess.

[21] Special Forces pattern of life monitoring often have an unrecognised but strategic impact upon operations.

[22] For example, the USAF employ the Reaper as primarily an Attack, Surveillance and Recce Platform while UK planning focuses on the persistent ISR capability with an Attack option.

[23] 'Reachback' to National facilities reduces deployed support costs while also allowing better use of limited analytical resource.

[24] FASOC – Para 37.

[25] There is no doubt that this issue will remain a constant challenge for Commanders delivering strategic effect.

[26] Urgent Operational Requirement – normally in response to changing threats or environments which require specialised equipment or additional capabilities.

[27] Canberra PR9, Nimrod Mk II, Tornado GR4.

[28] HLOC Commentary - Preface, para 3.

[29] August 08.

[30] Boeing and QinetiQ are currently in talks with US Defense Advanced Research Projects Agency (DARPA) to develop a UAV capable of staying airborne for 5 years while carrying a 1000lb payload.

[31] Tornado Integrated Avionics Research Aircraft - In Apr 07, QinetiQ completed a successful airborne demonstration of this capability. An F3 crew controlled a BAC 1-11 aircraft and 3 other surrogate UAV.

[32] Autonomous Systems Technology Related Airborne Evaluation and Assessment.

[33] Watchkeeper is destined to succeed H450 and is due to enter service in 2010. The acquisition of this platform has followed conventional MOD procurement processes.

[34] On 11 Sep 07, the US Senate Defense Appropriations Subcommittee approved the purchase of an additional 24 Predator and 5 Global Hawk UAV.

[35] As a minimum, there is at least one civil general air traffic incident/crash per week in the UK – the majority of these involve human error, yet there is no clamor to stop manned aviation. That is the UAV conundrum.

[36] UAV Frequency spectrum issues are on the agenda for WRC in 2011, however, this only addresses the issue of C2 for civilian/commercial air platforms.

[37] All air vehicles will be required to carry equipment that emits critical flight data. Given the recent advances in networked communications, GPS and mobile phone technologies, such a requirement should be affordable, reliable and fail-safe by 2020.

[38] We should not discount asymmetric attacks against key communication nodes which are based either on land or in space. Equally, as military dependence on

space grows, so will the vulnerability.

[39] A cruise missile flying for 3-4 hours against a fixed strategic targets conforms to LOAC, a UCAV on station for many days is less likely to meet such standards.

[40] Other vignettes could include NGO activities involving the Red Cross or the Media. Any autonomous system would need wide area data to understand the CDE implications of attacking a high value asset as it crossed a strategically important river dam.

[41] Equipment Capability – Deep Target Attack.

[42] Deep, Persistent, Offensive Capability.

[43] Launch and Recovery Element – Responsible for local air operations including take-off and recovery.

[44] On the assumption that a platform such as Global Hawk gathers unknown terabytes of ISR data, one wonders what percentage of this is properly catalogued and stored for future exploitation.

[45] The US Defense Advanced Research Projects Agency (DARPA) has launched an exploratory development program with the goal of placing a high-altitude, long endurance UAV anywhere on the planet within one hour, delivered by means of an intercontinental ballistic missile.

[46] DARPA are also funding an Expandable Local Area Sensors in a Tactically Interconnected Cluster (ELASTIC) initiative. This effort builds upon the dramatic gains in battlefield technology such as communications and cameras. They are planning to use systems with a power-consumption of no more than several hundred nanowatts to manage a network of sensors communicating sporadically to a mere milli-watt to deliver compressed FMV allowing for battery-powered sensors to survive for a considerable time.

[47] A soldier with a specific IP address could have the ability to view all (airborne) support assets within his local area of operation.

[48] Training Tactics and Procedures.

[49] Routinely, the MC could be expected to control a additional combat/attack platforms as well as his own.

[50] Circle of Error Probability.

[51] Although not addressed in this essay, the complexity of fusing numerous UAV/UCAV operations should not be underestimated. Data fusion and mission cohesion will depend upon resilient lines of communication and a clear understanding – both by CAOC staff and the MC - of mission aims and objectives.

[52] Scramble instruction, auto taxi and taxi-off, climb, descend, recovery, landing and auto taxi.

[53] Aug 07.

UNMANNED AERIAL VEHICLES – THE
LEGAL PERSPECTIVE

Wg Cdr Allison Mardell

The concept of a fully autonomous Unmanned Aerial Vehicle (UAV) would likely offer airpower a step change in capability. But is a fully autonomous UAV ever technologically feasible, especially when many of the legal implications of airpower, particularly the application of offensive force under the Laws of Armed Conflict (LOAC), are rarely black and white, even with a human decision-maker in the loop? Whilst the employment of these high-end, artificially intelligent, vehicles is technologically dubious (but not impossible), this certainly does not rule out the wider use of UAVs, at varying levels, on a sliding scale of autonomy. We have already seen the significant impact of UAVs on contemporary operations-witness the UK's contribution to Predator operations from the US-and undoubtedly the unmanned domain is here to stay. Therefore, not withstanding the aspirations to achieve full autonomy, the legal implications of operating UAVs are relevant now, as clearly there is a need to remain within the law as we continue UAV operations, both now and in the future. This paper, therefore, seeks to identify various potentially problematic legal issues concerning the operation of UAVs, in order to expose them and raise awareness of the possible implications they might have. These issues include autonomous capability and the application of LOAC; a discussion regarding the extent of legal liability of UAV operators; the possible use of civilians as operators of military UAVs and air space regulation and safety matters. It is hoped that the issues raised within this paper will provide a base line of information and opinion that will assist with the development of unmanned capabilities, not least the Unmanned Combat Aerial Vehicle (UCAV) and the policy for their employment.

Autonomous Uavs and the LOAC

The concept of 'autonomy' seems to have become increasingly synonymous with the development of UAVs. The recent press release[1] for Taranis from BAE Systems, for example, illustrates this preoccupation with autonomous capability and refers throughout to the UAV's autonomous ability and 'brains'. UAVs are not a new phenomenon, but their importance, development and use have increased significantly due in part to their ability to remove the human from harm's way during an attack. Technological advances have enabled UAVs to be used not only for traditional Intelligence Surveillance and Reconnaissance (ISR) tasking but also as a weapon system that can engage in attack; hence the distinction between UAV and UCAV. Using UAVs in either an ISR or attack capacity does not, by itself, contravene the Laws of Armed Conflict[2] (LOAC). It is only when one introduces the concept of an autonomous UCAV that controversies arise. This is because UCAVs can attack the enemy, either defensively[3] or offensively, through the use of armed force;

therefore, the provisions of LOAC, particularly concerning the protection of civilians and civilian objects during an armed conflict, will directly apply to the employment of UCAVs. The technology associated with autonomous capability of a UCAV, therefore, would need to facilitate compliance with the requirements of the LOAC if it is to be acceptable from a legal standpoint.

Arguably, there are two main areas that require consideration regarding the development of an autonomous capability for UCAVs. Firstly, what is meant by 'autonomy' in this context and, secondly, what considerations and decisions are required under LOAC prior to an attack. One needs to ask the latter question in order to ascertain what would be required of computer software if the human were removed from the decision cycle for an attack, even in part.

Autonomy should be viewed as a sliding scale. At the top of the scale will be a fully autonomous system that can do everything humans are required to do within LOAC, prior to and during an attack, including the ability to make the necessary decisions, and engage in the thought processes that this decision making involves. At the other end of the scale will be those systems that require human input in order for their use to comply with LOAC, but which may have some autonomous capability. For example, a weapon system that has an autonomous ability to identify and confirm an enemy target, without any human interference, but without being able to make any other decisions, such as where to search for the target in the first place, what weapon to use and whether to attack, has some autonomous capability but is not a fully autonomous system. In order for a fully autonomous system to be able to comply with LOAC, it must be able to make the qualitative assessments and decisions required under this area of law; or, put another way, the precautions in Article 57 must be capable of being taken, and while with a person in the loop this is easy to demonstrate (usually), the removal of that person from the crucial qualitative decisions (proportionality is a good example) means you have to ensure that the required precautions are taken somehow.

LOAC has developed exponentially over the last 150 years, gathering speed throughout the Twentieth Century, and particularly after WWII.[4] The main sources of LOAC are customary international law[5] and international treaties. Arguably, some of the most prominent milestones in treaty law have been the 4 Geneva Conventions of 1949[6] and the 2 Additional Protocols of 1977[7]; with Additional Protocol 1 (AP1)[8] adding significant detail to the 1949 Geneva Conventions, particularly in relation to the protection of civilians against the effects of hostilities. AP1 also introduced new definitions and most commentators would accept that AP1 has increased the obligations upon Parties to a conflict, particularly in relation to the protection of civilians, and a number of its Articles are now accepted as being declaratory of customary international law.[9] It is easy, when considering the rules and restrictions that the LOAC places on the warfighter, to overlook the spirit and intent behind the legal parameters. It cannot be doubted that one of the main reasons for the LOAC is to provide a system of protection for certain vulnerable categories of individuals and objects, that are not part of the direct warfighting machinery of the State, or combatants that have become hors de combat, but remain vulnerable to the fighting.

This raison d'être for the LOAC is demonstrated by the basic customary law principles of military necessity, distinction, proportionality and humanity. The principle of military necessity prescribes that Parties to an armed conflict are prohibited from engaging in destruction merely for destruction's sake. There must be a military reason why an attack is required against a particular object, and Parties must use only that level and type of force, not otherwise prohibited by the LOAC, which is necessary to achieve the objective of the conflict. It is now well established in treaty and customary law that civilians and civilian objects must not be made the object of attack.[10] In order to adhere to this principle and ensure, as far as possible, protection for the civilian population and civilian objects, Parties to a conflict must distinguish between civilians/civilian objects and combatants/military objectives to ensure, as far as possible, that only combatants and military objectives are attacked.[11] The principle of Proportionality[12] requires the number of expected civilian casualties or damage to civilian objects to be weighed against the military advantage anticipated from an attack. An attack will be lawful only when it is believed that the collateral damage would not be excessive in relation to the concrete and direct military advantage anticipated. In practice such decision-making is not easy since it is difficult to quantify a military advantage especially when judged against civilian loss of life or injury.[13] No matter how challenging the application of the principle of proportionality is, its application is imperative to ensure the lawful justification of each target. Once a military purpose has been achieved any further infliction of suffering in relation to that purpose will be unnecessary, and thus in breach of the military necessity principle. The principle of humanity additionally prescribes that parties to a conflict must not cause unnecessary suffering and superfluous injury. These basic principles of the LOAC now underpin the provisions contained in many treaties, specifically AP1. The UK ratified AP1 in 1998, and the Articles within AP1 in relation to the protection of the civilian population, namely Articles 48-58 inclusively, are generally accepted as having become declaratory of customary international law and, therefore, apply to all States regardless of whether they have ratified AP. However, there are some notable exceptions e.g. the US does not accept Article 55 regarding the protection of the environment nor does it accept Article 56 regarding the protection of dams, dykes etc; the US also blows hot and cold on the precise terms of the military objective definition. However, it is to AP1 that one must turn to determine much of the detail regarding the decisions and qualitative assessments required within the LOAC during the use of armed force.

There are clear requirements in AP1 for certain considerations and decisions to be made prior to an attack to ensure that the attack will be lawful. A number of these requirements are neatly summarised within Article 57 concerning precautions in attack. Article 57 reaffirms and draws together the overriding obligations placed upon the Parties to a conflict, in relation to the protection of the civilian population, and states as follows:

1.   *In the conduct of military operations, constant care shall be taken to spare the civilian population, civilians and civilian objects.*

2.   *With respect to attacks, the following precautions shall be taken:*

    (a)   Those who plan or decide upon an attack shall:

        (i)   do everything feasible to verify that the objectives to be attacked are neither civilians nor civilian objects and are not subject to special protection but are military objectives within the meaning of paragraph 2 of Article 52 and that it is not prohibited by the provisions of this Protocol to attack them;

        (ii) take all feasible precautions in the choice of means and methods of attack with a view to avoiding, and in any event to minimizing, incidental loss of civilian life, injury to civilians and damage to civilian objects;

        (iii) refrain from deciding to launch any attack which may be expected to cause incidental loss of civilian life, injury to civilians, damage to civilian objects, or a combination thereof, which would be excessive in relation to concrete and direct military advantage anticipated;

    (b)   an attack shall be cancelled or suspended if it becomes apparent that the objective is not a military one or is subject to special protection or that the attack may be expected to cause incidental loss of civilian life, injury to civilians, damage to civilian objects, or a combination thereof, that would be excessive in relation to the concrete and direct military advantage anticipated;

    (c)   effective advanced warning shall be given of attacks which may affect the civilian population, unless circumstances do not permit.

3.   *When a choice is possible between several military objectives for obtaining a similar military advantage, the objective to be selected shall be that the attack on which may be expected to cause the least danger to civilian life and civilian objects.*

4.   *In the conduct of military operations at sea or in the air, each party to the conflict shall, inconformity to it's rights and duties under the rules of international law applicable in armed conflict, take all reasonable precautions to avoid losses of civilian lives and damage to civilian objects.*

5.   *No provision of this article may be construed as authorizing any*

attacks against the civilian population, civilians or civilian objects.

Therefore, the first precaution required under Article 57(2)(a) is for the Parties to a conflict to do everything feasible to verify that the objectives to be attacked are not civilian or civilians, or objects subject to special protection.[14] This reaffirms the principle of distinction.[15] The second precaution is the requirement to use methods and means of warfare that avoid or minimise collateral damage and the third precaution introduces the proportionality principle. Also of significance is the requirement in Article 57(2)(b) to cancel or suspend an attack under certain circumstances.[16] Therefore, a decision is required regarding the verification of the targets to be attacked, how each target is to be attacked to avoid or minimise collateral damage, whether the attack would be proportionate and whether due, for example, to new information or change in circumstances, the attack should be cancelled or suspended. Also, where there are several targets that if attacked individually would provide a similar military advantage, there is the requirement within Article 57(3) to choose the target that is likely to cause the least amount of collateral damage if attacked. For a UCAV to be fully autonomous it would have to be capable of considering these precautions and deciding upon the appropriate actions to take. For example, it would have to be able to determine the likely amount of collateral damage that may be caused from an attack and determine whether the military advantage anticipated from the attack would justify that amount of collateral damage.

LOAC does not specify that decision making must be carried out by humans, therefore, providing the relevant decisions are made, it does not seem to matter whether this process is undertaken by humans or machines. Article 57(2)(a) does not refer to a specific decision maker, but refers to 'those' who decide upon an attack. This could include any person who at some stage may have the ability and authority, to make a decision regarding the prosecution of an attack. This will, of course, include the commander who may authorise the attack, but the ability and authority may also may fall to the troops on the ground or in the air who actually carry out the attack: those who actually fire a rifle or release a bomb. When Article 57 was drafted there was much debate[17] about the scope of the phrase "those who plan or decide upon an attack", particularly regarding who it was meant to include. Some argued it placed too much responsibility on subordinates and that it should only apply to commanding officers. However, many others recognised that, in some fighting, especially in circumstances of timeliness, decisions would be taken at the lowest level and this provision needed to cover all eventualities in order for the precautions to be effective. Certainly planners and commanders will fall into this category but so may others who, due to the circumstances, have some discretion regarding the way the attack is carried out.[18]

Depending on the circumstances, therefore, there may be several decision makers, at different levels, in one kill chain. The same reasoning also applies to those who plan the attack; all those involved in this regard bear the responsibility to consider and take the precautions listed within Article 57, including the concomitant decisions that have to be made which are integral to compliance. Whilst this may seem a wide interpretation to some, arguably it is the only one that allows 'constant care' to be taken, as required under Article 57(1). If the line of responsibility to comply with these precautions was drawn at a particular level of command, it would allow the precautions to be ignored at all other levels, thereby diluting the protection meant for civilians.

However, recognition of the reality of conflict, particularly the fact that people can only do so much in difficult circumstances and within the bounds of technology, is acknowledged through the inclusion of the word 'feasible'. The UK has interpreted 'feasible' to mean "that which is practicable or practically possible, taking into account all circumstances ruling at the time, including humanitarian and military considerations."[19] Therefore, there will come the point at which time it will not be possible under the circumstances to take any more care, but the acceptable threshold, in relation to the precautions, must have been reached for the attack to be lawful.

The UK adopted the same pragmatic approach, in relation to Article 57(2)(b), when it included the following statement of interpretation upon ratification of AP1:

> "The UK understands that the obligation to comply with paragraph 2(b) only extends to those who have the authority and practical possibility to cancel or suspend the attack."

However, this statement should not be interpreted as an attempt to usurp the provisions of AP1, by encouraging the development of technology that is not capable of cancelling or suspending an attack, in order to argue that, as it is not 'practically possible' to take this precaution, the requirement to do so is removed. Rather it should be interpreted as an attempt to incorporate the reality of war fighting into the interpretation of AP1. For example, in some circumstances, despite all precautions being taken prior to an attack, once a weapon system has been released, like a ballistic missile, it would not be practically possible to suspend or cancel that attack, however, it is still necessary to take all of the precautions prior to the release of the weapon. Therefore, developing a weapon system that cannot take precautions is not the answer, because if the system cannot take the precautions the requirement to do so does not disappear, the human will have to take them, until it is no longer feasible to do so. The point is that the 'one way missile' makes no decision and is fired by a human at a target chosen by a human who knows when it may be expected to hit it and who has considered all available target specific information and made the necessary qualitative evaluations, if the autonomous UCAV removes the human from these activities the issue is whether it achieves them itself.

As well as the precautions within Article 57 of AP1, there are also other rules within LOAC that require qualitative decisions during an attack. For example, the requirement under Article 41 of AP1 not to attack those who have been recognised as hors de combat or as surrendering, or who, under the circumstances, should have been recognised as such. A fully autonomous system would have to be capable of recognising those who were hors de combat or who had surrendered in order to maintain the protection intended for these categories of person. Of course the system may not be operating alone. There may be other systems securing awareness of what is going on in the target area and which may ensure compliance with the precautions requirement. Or, the nature of the search area may enable those who plan the attack to have a sufficient level of assurance that collateral risks can be obviated – remote land areas, seas, deserts etc. If the weapon system could not distinguish combatants from surrendered combatants, then a human would be required to monitor the battle space in order to identify surrendered combatants etc, or another mechanical system that can do this may be usable.

As referred to above, there are already weapon systems that have a certain amount of autonomous capability, but remain reliant upon the 'human in the loop' to comply with the requirements under LOAC. For example, the autonomous element of Brimstone is the ability, through its sensor, to seek out, identify and attack the enemy target. The group of objects at which the pilot fires is the composite target and therefore he the pilot or the planners do the proportionality etc checks before it is fired at the composite target and the individual search just makes it more discriminating.

Once an appropriate target set has been detected in a particular area, Brimstone is programmed, by a human, to start its search at a particular point within the search area, end its search at particular point and then, if it fails to find a target within this area, it is programmed, again by a human, to self-destruct at a particular point. Therefore, the target and its position will have been identified and determined beforehand by a human, and the search area and destruction point will be calculated and determined by a human. In relation to the precautions under LOAC, the target will have been verified by humans upon detection; it is designed to search a limited area for a specific target and self destruct in a pre-programmed and benign area, all controlled by humans, thereby complying with the principle of discrimination; and the proportionality and collateral damage implications of the attack will have been considered by humans beforehand, or by the pilot in the cockpit. Brimstone's autonomous capability is the ability to search the area and find the target, by which I mean locate a pre-designated target group, and attack. Therefore, through a mixture of machine and man, all precautions will have been met.

Due to the current limitations of technology, it seems that a fully autonomous system is still an aspiration, but some autonomous capabilities have been and are still being developed, albeit that human input is still required in order to comply with LOAC. The level of human input will depend not only upon the level of technology but also confidence in that technology. For example, with Taranis, BAE Systems claim to have developed a system that can "autonomously control the aircraft to taxi, take off and navigate its way to a search area while reacting to any threats or other events. It will then route its way around the search area in whichever way it wants, to locate the target and then use its sensor system to transmit a series of images and views back to the operator to confirm that it is the target to be attacked. Then, once it has been authorised to do so, it autonomously attacks that target, routes its way back home, lands and taxis back."[20] Whilst this system may be able to act autonomously in the ways described, it is still a long way from having the level of 'artificial intelligence' required to address the qualitative decisions required under LOAC. For example, the human is still required to monitor the imagery, identify the target, assess the expected collateral damage and authorise the attack.

A further issue to consider is the actual benefit a fully autonomous UCAV can bring to the warfighter. Arguably it removes the human, or at least the human aircrew, from harm's way and it may limit the scope for human error. However, this must be weighed against the amount of confidence in the autonomous system to always function correctly and the possibility of its decision process being affected by the environment e.g. extreme weather conditions or jamming by the enemy. Also, in some circumstances humans may be better able to respond to the dynamic environment of an armed conflict with initiative and agility that would be extremely difficult, if not impossible, to replicate in a machine. A better approach may be to concentrate on how degrees of autonomy within weapon systems can enhance the capability of the warfighter, not least of all by removing him or her from the immediate danger of the front line, as opposed to concentrating on removing him or her completely from the decision process. However, In some circumstances an autonomous system may be able to cope better than a human for example in situations of extreme pressure where a decision is required in seconds, whilst in other circumstances human intuition, flexibility and experience may eclipse any benefit the autonomous system has to offer. Currently, in relation to compliance with the LOAC the human remains an integral part of the decision making process, and will do so, until such time that technology produces sufficient 'artificial intelligence' for a autonomous system to comply with the decisions required to ensure an attack is lawful under the LOAC.

Legal Liability and UAV Operations

There are different types of liability in law e.g. criminal liability and tortious liability; each requiring the presence of different elements before legal liability attaches to an individual. Whether an individual will be liable in law for either a crime or a tort will always depend on the facts of each case and whether the elements of the crime or tort can be established.

The following is a simple example illustrating the way that different circumstances can alter the responsibility, and potential liability, for a decision. If a pilot is given a fixed target from the Air Tasking Order (ATO) he must rely on the fixed targeting process, and it would be reasonable for him to expect others, namely those involved in the targeting cycle, to have verified the target, ensured its lawfulness and have produced accurate co-ordinates etc. If, for example, the co-ordinates turn out to be incorrect and a civilian object is hit, and there is no evidence to show that the pilot should have realised that the co-ordinates were incorrect, then the pilot will not bare responsibility for the incident; responsibility will lie elsewhere, even though it is not with the person who actually released the weapon. The individual who produced the wrong co-ordinates may have been negligent or, if he or she intended the consequences that occurred through providing the wrong co-ordinates, may be criminally liable. Of course, if the pilot is in a position to visually identify the target, or has enough information or situational awareness to raise his or her concern regarding the target, then he or she must be satisfied that it is appropriate to release the weapon. In short, if the pilot has doubts, he must resolve these first and only attack when the military status of the target is clear. Where a Forward Air Controller (FAC) is engaged, then he or she will usually be in a better position than the pilot to assess a threat and identify a target and apply LOAC, whereupon the pilot will rely on the FAC's judgement and the responsibility for weapon release will lie with the latter. However, if the pilot can see something that the FAC cannot, for example, civilians sheltering behind a building out of view of the FAC, but who will be caught up in the attack, the onus then shifts to the pilot to act accordingly upon this information. Therefore, who bears responsibility for the decision, and whether any legal liability flows from that decision, will depend on facts of the incident and who was involved. Indeed, there may be several people that bear responsibility for one incident.[21]

Of course, a person may be responsible for a decision or activity that causes harm or damage but, due to the circumstances, may not bear any liability in law. In relation to the application of LOAC, an individual's actions will not be judged in hindsight, but with regard to the circumstances at the time of the incident, including the pressure they were under and the information they had at the time. This is confirmed by the following statement of understanding to AP1 made by the UK:

> "Military commanders and others responsible for planning, deciding upon or executing attacks necessarily have to reach decisions on the basis of their assessment of the information from all sources which is reasonably available to them at the relevant time."

During an armed conflict concerns in relation to legal liability usually centre on individual criminal liability for war crimes. Whether a person will be criminally liable for a war crime will depend on the circumstances surrounding each case and the nature of the alleged crime. Military UCAV operators will be subject to the same criminal law, both domestic and international, as any other combatant and must, therefore, comply with LOAC.

The following are examples of war crimes to illustrate the nature and scope of criminal issues that may arise as a result of attacks against the enemy. The 4 Geneva Conventions of 1949 list several 'grave breaches' which if committed may amount to a war crime; these war crimes were incorporated into the UK's domestic legislation through the enactment of the Geneva Convention Act 1957. Article 85, within AP1, adds to the list of war crimes, and, inter alia, refers specifically to Article 57:

"…The following acts shall be regarded as grave breaches of this Protocol, when committed wilfully, in violation of the relevant provisions of this Protocol, causing death or serious injury to body or health:

> (a)   *making the civilian population or individual civilians the object of attack;*

> (b)   *launching an indiscriminate attack affecting the civilian population or civilian objects in the knowledge that such attack will cause excessive loss of life, injury to civilians or damage to civilian objects, as defined in Article 57, paragraph 2 (a) (iii);*

> (c)   *launching an attack against works or installations containing dangerous forces in the knowledge that such an attack will cause excessive loss of life, injury to civilians or damage to civilian objects, as defined in Article 57, paragraph 2 (a) (iii);…"*

The 1993 Statute establishing the International Criminal Tribunal for the Former Yugoslavia (ICTY) lists, inter alia, as grave breaches of the Geneva Conventions the following:

> *"… extensive destruction and appropriation of property, not justified by military necessity and carried out unlawfully and wantonly… the wanton destruction of cities, towns or villages, or devastation not justified by military necessity; attack or bombardment, by whatever means of undefended towns, villages, dwellings or buildings."*

Finally, the war crimes within the 1998 Rome Statute for the International Criminal Court (Rome Statute) are listed as those "Grave breaches of the Geneva Conventions of 12th August 1949" and include: wilful killing; extensive destruction and appropriation of property, not justified by military necessity and carried out unlawfully and wantonly; intentionally directing attacks against the civilian population as such or against individual civilians not taking a direct part in hostilities; intentionally directing attacks against civilian objects that is, objects which are not military objectives; intentionally launching an attack in the knowledge that such attack will cause incidental loss of life or injury to civilians or damage to civilian objects or widespread, long term and severe damage to the natural environment which would be clearly excessive in relation to the concrete and direct overall military advantage anticipated ; attacking or bombarding, by whatever means, towns, villages, dwellings or buildings which are undefended and are not military objectives; killing or wounding a combatant who, having laid down his arms or having no longer means of defence, has surrendered at discretion.[22]

A constant element within the war crimes listed above is the requirement that they are committed 'intentionally', 'wantonly', 'wilfully' or 'with knowledge'. Therefore, in most cases, to be guilty of a war crime, the perpetrator must have intended to bring about the consequences that have resulted from his actions;

which is more than just being reckless or negligent. 'Intention' is the highest threshold in relation to the mental element required for a criminal offence, and therefore, often the most difficult to establish. Individual criminal liability for a war crime contingent upon the perpetrator of the offence having the intention to commit the act that amounts to the crime.

In practice, therefore, if a commander, or those who plan an attack, decide upon an attack or execute an attack do all that is practical in the circumstances to gather and review the intelligence available to them and conclude in good faith that the object of attack is a legitimate military target and have done everything practicable to avoid or minimise collateral damage, then they will have complied with the LOAC.[23] Providing they have acted in good faith, based on the information available to them at the time, they will be able to justify their actions and decisions.[24] Of course one should remember that not all breaches of the LOAC will amount to a war crime, such breaches, however, may still have a significant impact on the individual, and strategically in relation to the operational campaign; the most obvious example being media and public opinion.

The principles discussed above, regarding war crimes, will apply to the employment of weapons from a UCAV in the same way as they apply to the employment of any other lawful weapon system. In relation to an autonomous UCAV, or a UCAV that has some element of autonomous capability, its characteristics and limitations will need to be understood by its operator to ensure that it is used in compliance with the LOAC. A level of confidence must have already been reached in relation to the autonomous element of the system, for example through successful trials – meaning that it must be capable of being used in such a way as allows of the precautions in attack required by the law; the human input must then reach the threshold required by the LOAC. Even with a fully autonomous UCAV the actual decision to use it at a particular place and time within the battle may still have to be made by a human, who will be responsible for that decision and may at a later date have to explain and justify it.

Civilians as Military UAV Operators

Given that many UAVs will allow operators to be removed from the battlefield and be placed out of harm's way, this might raise the question of whether UAV operators need to be combatants or whether civilians can undertake this role. The most obvious legal issue regarding the use of civilians in this role is the application of the LOAC in relation to the protection of civilians and the circumstances that give rise to the loss of this protection. As referred to above, under the LOAC, civilians cannot be made the object of attack. However, in the same way as civilian objects can become military objectives, civilians can loose their protected status "for such time as they take a direct part in hostilities."[25] Unfortunately, the phrase "direct part in hostilities" has never been clarified in treaty law and has consequently been subject to differing interpretations and resultant controversy.

Whilst it is not unlawful in itself for civilians to play a direct part in hostilities, there are certain consequences that flow from such activity. The first consequence is that their immunity from attack will be lost for such time as they so participate and the civilian or civilians involved can be made the object of attack; if captured by the enemy they may not (levee) be entitled to prisoner of war status, as they will not be recognised combatants, they will remain as civilians who have lost their protective status; and finally, they may also be subject to criminal prosecution if their 'direct part in hostilities' amounts to a criminal offence e.g. murder is it worth spelling out that any intentional causing of a death that is not self defence is likely to be murder. Therefore, allowing civilians to operate UAVs during armed conflict may have significant implications for them if their activity amounts to a direct part in hostilities.

Looking at the varying interpretations of 'direct part in hostilities',[26] the commentary for AP1 states that the behaviour of civilians must constitute a direct and immediate military threat to the adversary, before it can be said they are playing a direct part in hostilities. If 'direct participation' is required then 'indirect participation' must be acceptable. Whilst neither is a war crime as such, it is important therefore to establish the fault line between direct and indirect participation, but what activity constitutes either? If the term 'hostilities' is interpreted too widely (i.e. any activity that may help the enemy) this may remove the protection for civilians in many circumstances, significantly eroding their protection. However, if it is interpreted too narrowly, it may prevent the military from taking sufficient measures to counter threats or activities from the civilian population. For example, should 'hostilities' include the activities of civilians engaged in the collection of materials to donate to the war effort e.g. tin cans. f it were to include such activities then any other similar activity, carried out by civilians, aimed at helping the war effort in general, could amount to a direct part in hostilities, thereby usurping much of the protection intended for civilians during an armed conflict. Arguably, this type of activity can be categorised as an 'indirect activity' and merely 'war sustaining', not a direct and immediate military threat, therefore, should not be included within a definition of hostilities. It has been suggested that 'hostilities' should only include activities that are intended to actually cause harm and destruction as opposed to activities that only develop the capacity to do so.[27] Arguably, civilians are allowed to support their armed forces in times of conflict, for example, by sending food parcels to deployed troops or being engaged in making military ration packs[28], without losing their protected status?

However, at the other end of the scale, it can be safely argued that civilians actually engaged in an attack, thereby physically fighting the enemy, are playing a direct part in hostilities. There remains, however, a grey area of activity, which supports the military but is short of actual fighting. For example, civilians involved in logistical support or intelligence collection for the military, or guarding either a military unit or prisoner of war camp. There is also debate about the exact duration of taking a direct part in hostilities. For example, does such participation start when the attack is being planned and end when the attacker reaches safety, or does direct participation in hostilities only last during the actual attack which causes a threat to the adversary?

The discussion above demonstrates the ambiguity that characterises the notion of 'taking a direct part in hostilities'. In relation to the civilian operation of UCAVs during an armed conflict one could successfully argue that this will amount to 'taking a direct part in hostilities', as it would include a direct and immediate threat to the enemy. However, could civilian contractors legitimately launch the vehicle and pass it to a military controller to fly to the combat zone? While deployment forward clearly is 'taking a direct part in hostilities', I am not sure that the launching necessarily is, but it may depend on the nature of the machine. Perhaps launching is 'taking a direct part in hostilities' if, once launched, the machine flies itself to its zone of operations. An area of even less certainty is the status of civilian UAV operators engaged in ISR tasking. There is a divergence of views in this regard as it falls squarely into the 'grey area' referred to above. On the one hand some argue that intelligence gathering is not directly related to an attack and therefore, does not amount to hostilities; and on the other, some argue that intelligence gathering has a direct connection to the ability to attack or defend, and therefore falls within scope of playing a direct part in hostilities.[29]   Whatever the UK's interpretation, however, there will always be the risk that the enemy adopts a wide interpretation and includes ISR tasking as playing a direct part in hostilities, and will therefore view civilians engaged in such activity as lawful objects of attack.

Any proposal to use civilians as UAV operators, therefore, should take into account the likely risk to them, particularly in relation to the loss of immunity from attack. It is accepted that the risk to the operators in this regard may be slight where they are thousands of miles from the area of operations at a home base in relative safety; however, this may not always be the case, and there is always the possibility of the enemy attacking UK territory. There is also the risk that by employing civilians in ambiguous roles, the wider protection of them may be compromised, not least if confusion as to who is and who is not participating in the hostilities is created.

Air Space Regulation and Safety Standards

The safety and operational standards for UAV flights is a major issue, therefore, this brief outline of the body of rules governing the use of airspace is intended to highlight the potential difficulties associated with UAVs and flying regulations.

Since the introduction of the Paris Convention in 1919, a number of international treaties[30] and institutions[31] have been created that provide comprehensive regulations and oversight of the use of airspace.[32] The main Treaty in relation to civilian aircraft is the Chicago Convention 1944 on International Civil Aviation (Chicago Convention).[33] As a signatory of the Chicago Convention and member of the International Civil Aviation Organisation (ICAO), the UK undertakes to comply with the provisions of the Chicago Convention and its Annexes. However, Article 3 of the Chicago Convention stipulates that it only applies to civil aircraft and not to State aircraft. State aircraft are defined as those aircraft used in military, customs and police services.[34] Therefore, the MOD has been left to develop its own regulatory standards in relation to military aircraft. This has resulted in the development of 2 regulatory regimes within the UK: civilian and military.

The military regime within the UK is governed by the Ministry of Defence (MOD), which has produced JSP 550, the Military Aviation Policy Regulations and Directives, and JSP 553, the Military Airworthiness Regulations. The main civilian requirements for the UK are set out in the Air Navigation Order 2005 (ANO) and the rules of the Air Regulations 2006 (both fall under the Civil Aviation Act 1982). As referred to above, the majority of national civil aviation legislation does not apply to UK military aircraft. However, MOD policy is to provide military regulations that correspond to the civilian rules, and to ensure the same effective level of regulation to the regulations contained within the ANO. The policy of the Civil Aviation Authority (CAA) is that UAVs operating in the UK must meet the same or better safety and operational standards as manned aircraft 'in so far as they must not present or create a hazard to persons or property in the air or on the ground greater than that attributable to the operations of manned aircraft'.[35] This has been mirrored by MOD policy, which supports the view that military UAVs must show an equivalent level of compliance with the regulations for manned aircraft.

At present, to ensure that the equivalent level of safety to that required for manned flying is achieved, UAV operations are restricted to segregated airspace. Currently, there are no national procedures that permit either civil or military UAVs to routinely fly in non-segregated airspace. One of the main areas of concern surrounding UAVs seems to be their ability, or lack of ability, to 'sense and avoid' other aircraft. At present the CAA require a similar ability for UAVs to 'sense and avoid' as achieved by manned aircraft, which remains a technological issue. Arguably, therefore, it is unlikely that UAVs will be allowed to fly routinely in segregated airspace until they reach the same threshold of 'see and avoid' capability, equivalent to that reached by manned aircraft. This of course is likely to have a number of implications regarding the development of UAVs in general as well as the ability to train personnel to operate UAVs and acquire flying experience. However, given their proven utility, I have no doubt that, within time, the civilian and military authorities, with the assistance of technology, will reached a solution that may ultimately allow the routine flight of UAVs within UK airspace.

Conclusion

The utility of UAVs, in particular their ability to remove the human from harm's way and provide increased persistence, means that they are here to stay. The aspiration for a fully autonomous UCAV may not be technically? possible today but systems are already being developed with levels of autonomous capability. The autonomous capability being planned for Taranis, for example, may enhance operational effectiveness by removing the more mundane considerations from the human, allowing more concentration on complex decisions, however, the human must still remain 'in the loop', to verify and authorise the attack. A fully autonomous system would have to be capable of making the qualitative assessments currently required by LOAC, until this is possible the human must remain within the decision-making process. The law applies to UAV and UCAV operators in exactly the same way as it applies to all other military personnel operating different weapon systems, therefore, UAV and UCAV operators must understand the characteristics and capabilities of the system they are operating to ensure that these systems are used appropriately and in accordance with the law.

Whether or not consideration will be given to using civilians as UAV and UCAV operators remains to be seen, but if it is, then the possible consequences for those civilians under LOAC must be borne in mind. Civilians operators used during an armed conflict are likely to loose their protected status, and will definitely do so if operating a UCAV that is in the combat zone or deploying to or from it. They may also face criminal prosecution if captured by the enemy and will have no right to PW status. We could certainly be criticised as a State for placing civilians in such a precarious position.

Finally, progress with the development of UAVs and training may be hindered by the current approach to UAV flights in UK airspace. However, once the technology for 'sense and avoid' capability for UAVs is accepted it is likely that the regulations may be relaxed allowing more routine UAV flights and the increased acceptance of their presence in our skies.

Without doubt UAVs are here to stay, and if we wish to take advantage of increasingly sophisticated technology, perhaps resulting in full autonomy, then throughout the development of any UAV capability we must be mindful of the very real constraints that legal requirements can place upon these capabilities. These constraints are not necessarily insurmountable but currently it would appear we are still some way off.

NOTES

[1] 18 Jun 2007/ Ref. 178/2007 'UK Taranis UAV Passes First Major Milestone'.
[2] The title of the Law of Armed Conflict (LOAC) and International Humanitarian Law (IHL) refer to the same body of law.
[3] Article 49 AP1 defines 'attacks' as 'acts of violence against the adversary whether in offence or in defence'. 'Defence' was included to make the scope and application of AP1 as wide as possible. Article 49 continues to state that 'The provisions of this protocol with respect to attacks apply to all attacks in whatever territory conducted, including the national territory belonging to a Party to the conflict but under the control of an adverse Party'.
[4] A number of important treaties were ratified prior to WWII including, for

example, the 1868 St Petersburg Declaration, viewed as the first major international Treaty prohibiting the use of a particular weapon during warfare, namely explosive projectiles under 400 grams of weight; the 1907 Hague Convention IV Respecting the Laws and Customs of War on Land, still relevant today; and the 1925 Geneva Protocol for the Prohibition of the Use in War of Asphyxiating, Poisonous or Other Gases, and of Bacteriological Methods of Warfare.

[5] Customary law develops through State practice and is created when extensive State practice exists together with *Opinio Juris*: the belief by States that there is a legal obligation or right to act in a particular way. All States are bound by customary international law, whereas only those States that ratify a Treaty are bound by the terms of the Treaty, unless provisions within a treaty have also crystallized into customary international law.

[6] 1949 Geneva Convention I for the Amelioration of the Condition of the Wounded and Sick in Armed Forces in the Field: 1949 Geneva Convention II for the Amelioration of the Condition of the Wounded, Sick and Shipwrecked Members of Armed Forces at Sea: 1949 Geneva Convention III Relative to the Treatment of Prisoners of War: 1949 Geneva Convention IV Relative to the Protection of Civilians in Time of War.

[7] 1977 Geneva Protocol I Additional to the Geneva Conventions of 12 August 1949, and Relating to the Protection of Victims of International Armed Conflicts (AP1) and 1977 Geneva Protocol II Additional to the Geneva Conventions of 12 August 1949, and Relating to the Protection of Victims of Non-International Armed Conflicts (AP1I).

[8] The UK ratified AP1 on 28 January 1998.

[9] See Parks, W. Hayes, 'Air War and the Law of War', the Air Force Law Review, Volume 32, Number 1, 1990 - Hays' point within this article is that certain of the obligations in the Protocol are inappropriate for the reasons he explains, and his argument now is that a number of the AP1 provisions are not customary law.

[10] This is confirmed in the recent study by the International Committee of the Red Cross (ICRC), see Henckaerts, Jean-Marie, Doswald-Beck, Louise, 'Customary International Humanitarian Law', ICRC, Cambridge University Press. However, civilians and civilian objects may be attacked under certain circumstances. Civilian objects may become legitimate targets if they fall within the definition of military objectives found in Article 52 (2) of AP1 which states that "Attacks should be limited strictly to military objectives. In so far as objects are concerned, military objectives are limited to those objects which by their nature, location, purpose or use make an effective contribution to military action and whose total or partial destruction, capture or neutralisation, in the circumstances ruling at the time, offers a definite military advantage." Civilians may be attacked if they lose their protected status 'for such time as they take a direct part in hostilities' (Article 51(3) of AP1). There is also the question of reprisals.

[11] The principle of distinction is now codified in article 48 of AP1, which states as follows: "In order to ensure respect for the protection of the civilian population and civilian objects, the Parties to the conflict shall at all times distinguish between the civilian population and combatants and between civilian objects

and military objectives and accordingly shall direct their operations only against military objectives."

[12] Article 57 (2) (b) of AP1 states that "An attack shall be cancelled or suspended if it becomes apparent that the object is not a military one or is subject to special protection or that the attack may be expected to cause incidental loss of civilian life, injury to civilians, damage to civilian objects, or a combination thereof, which would be excessive in relation to the concrete and direct military advantage anticipated."

[13] The Committee established to review the NATO bombing campaign against the Federal Republic of Yugoslavia confirmed that the 'determination of relative values' in relation to proportionality must be that of the 'reasonable military commander'. Therefore, the question to be addressed by decision makers prior to an attack is: would a reasonable military commander, under the circumstances at the time of the attack, have considered that the expected damage to civilians/civilian objects was proportionate to the expected military advantage?

[14] Within AP1 Articles 53, 54, 55 and 56 gives special protection from attack to cultural objects, objects indispensable to the survival of the civilian population, the natural environment and works and installations containing dangerous forces.

[15] The principle of distinction is reaffirmed in Article 48 of AP1 as follows: "In order to ensure respect for and protection of the civilian population and civilian objects, the parties to the conflict shall at all times distinguish between the civilian population and combatants and between civilian objects and military objectives and accordingly shall direct their operations only against military objectives."

[16] Upon ratification of AP1 the UK entered the following statement of interpretation in relation to Article 57, AP1: "The UK understands that the obligation to comply with paragraph 2(b) only extends to those who have the authority and practical possibility to cancel or suspend the attack."

[17] See Y Sandoz, C Swinarski, and B Zimmerman (eds) 'Commentary on the Additional Protocols of 8 June 1977 to the Geneva Conventions of 12 August 1949', (1987).

[18] This is also the view adopted in the JSP 383 – 'The Joint Service Manual of the Law of Armed Conflict' 2004 Edition.

[19] Taken from one the 16 statements of interpretation the UK made before it ratified AP1.

[20] 18 Jun 2007/ Ref. 178/2007 'UK Taranis UAV Passes First Major Milestone'.

[21] Art 3 to Hague IV 1907.

[22] These are just some examples that appear the most relevant to this particular matter, there are many more crimes listed within the Geneva Conventions and Rome Statute.

[23] This of course is the issue if the technology prevents them from doing something that perhaps less sophisticated technology would permit!

[24] There are other areas of liability that a person may be subject to, even though they don't have the sufficient intent to have committed a war crime, for example, they may have committed a military offence, namely, 'negligently performing a

duty', or there actions may justify administrative action.

[25] Article 51(3) of AP1.

[26] To assist in this area a series of Expert Meetings co-organised by the ICRC and the TMC Asser Institute are endeavouring to clarify the precise meaning of the notion of "direct part in hostilities.

[27] See the Third Expert Meeting on the Notion of Direct Participation in Hostilities, Summary Report, Oct 2005.

[28] A facility used for the production of military ration packs could be attacked as a military objective, but individual civilians working in the facility could not be attacked unless this type of activity was viewed as amounting to playing a direct part in hostilities.

[29] See the Third Expert Meeting on the Notion of Direct Participation in Hostilities, Summary Report, Oct 2005.

[30] For example the Warsaw Convention 1929 for the Unification of Certain Rules Relating to International Carriage by Air (Warsaw Convention); the Chicago Convention 1944 on International Civil Aviation; Tokyo Convention1963 on Offences and Certain Other Acts Committed on Board Aircraft (Tokyo Convention); the Montreal Convention 1999 for the Unification of Certain Rules for International Carriage by Air (Montreal Convention 1999).

[31] For example the International Civil Aviation Organisation (ICAO), a Specialised Agency of the United Nations pursuant to Article 64 of the Chicago Convention; the International Air Transport Association (IATA), a private organisation of scheduled airlines and the European Aviation Safety Agency (EASA) formed under EC Regulation 1592/2002 and for national regulation the Civil Aviation Authority (CAA).

[32] Article 1 of the Chicago Convention states that 'every State has complete and exclusive sovereignty over the airspace above its territory.' At present there is no internationally accepted definition of airspace and many States have tended to adopt a practical view of the extent of airspace, for example JSP 383 'The Joint Service Manual of the Law of Armed Conflict' provides that 'For practical purposes, it can be said that the upper limit to a state's rights in airspace is above the highest altitude at which an aircraft can fly and below the lowest possible perigee of an earth satellite in orbit.' Aircraft have freedom of overflight in 'international airspace' which comprises exclusive economic zones and airspace over the high seas.

[33] It should be noted that Article 8 of the Chicago Convention states that no aircraft capable of being flown without a pilot shall be flown over the territory of a contracting State without special authorisation of that State.

[34] Article 3b of the Chicago Convention.

[35] UAV aerial vehicle operations – guidance CAP722.

UNMANNED AERIAL VEHICLES – CULTURAL ISSUES

Mr Seb Cox

HIGH FLIGHT

Oh I have slipped the surly bonds of earth
And danced the skies on laughter-silvered wings;
Sunward I've climbed, and joined the tumbling mirth
Of sun-split clouds – and done a hundred things
You have not dreamed of – wheeled and soared and swung
High in the sunlit silence. Hov'ring there
I've chased the shouting wind along, and flung,
My eager craft through footless halls of air.
Up, up the long, delirious burning blue
I've topped the windswept heights with easy grace
Where never lark, or even eagle flew.
And, while with silent, lifting mind I've trod
The high untrespassed sanctity of space,
Put out my hand, and touched the hand of God

P/O John Gillespie Magee Jr [1922-1941][1]

"What's the Difference between God and pilots? God doesn't think he's a pilot."

Anon[2]

The oft-quoted poem High Flight, written by RCAF Spitfire pilot John Gillespie Magee epitomises the joy and freedom of flight. It is also a metaphor for escape from earthbound cares, the "surly bonds" of humdrum existence. Written in the first person, it explicitly links flying to Heaven and to God, and implicitly links the activity to a superior existence accessible only to a few – "a hundred things *you* have not dreamed of...". It is, in other words, unashamedly elitist: the airman really can reach out and touch the face of God, where others cannot. The anonymous quote that follows on the other hand is surely written by a non-pilot; be he a long-suffering engineer, navigator or perhaps met man.

Yet both speak to the image of the aviator, and especially the pilot. The spoken or unspoken assumption of superiority; of a natural order of things in which pilots are the only ones who matter. This is not simply a reflection of the personality-types who join the Air Forces as pilots (although that may raise a smile amongst non-pilots), but also a reflection of a simple historical truth. From the start of the First World War until today only a very small cadre of the RAF, and its predecessors the Royal Flying Corps and the Royal Naval

Air Service, have actually fought. On 1st May 1945, a week before the Second World War in Europe came to an end, there were 144488 aircrew [all men] in the RAF compared with 988827 men and women in "ground trades". Of the total strength of 1,133315 men and women approximately one in eight [12.75%] were therefore aircrew. However, only 73,897 aircrew were fully trained, compared to 815540 trained groundcrew of 831541 in total [excluding women]. The percentage of the trained manpower strength of the RAF who were aircrew was therefore less than 10% [9.06]. Of these 26556 were pilots, or 2.3% of the total trained manpower.[3]

The above figures relate to all aircrew. On 1st July 1945 [no data is available for May] there were 40973 pilots in the RAF. Of these 41000 men, 12000 or 29% were in operational units. The total male strength of the RAF at that point was 940867 so only 1.3% of men in the RAF were pilots in frontline units. Yet historically it is men from this statistically very small pilot-aircrew segment of the service who have dominated the upper echelons of the Royal Air Force. There has never been a Chief of the Air Staff in the entire ninety year history of the RAF who was not a pilot, never mind an airman. A handful of navigators have made it to the highest ranks, but never to CAS, and a few engineers have also served on the Air Force Board, but always in a technically-related post. This also represents a much narrower "gene-pool" from which to draw than a comparable percentage of say "teeth-arms" officers in the Army from which the CGS is traditionally drawn. This is not an historical accident. Both services perceive that the head of the service must be from the combat arm and the perception is that this is the only background that can give the necessary credibility to lead an *armed* service. This, however, does *not* fully explain why non-pilot aircrew have so consistently failed to attain the highest positions in the RAF. In fact there is little logic in this position. It is, however, a prejudice of long-standing and a persistent one. In the early years of the Royal Flying Corps it was assumed that Observers would all eventually want to become pilots and that their status as what would now be termed "backseaters" (though in some early aircraft the observer sat in front of the pilot) was merely temporary. The fact that many of the primary missions of the RFC required higher levels of skill from the observer than they did the pilot was largely ignored. Indeed, as late as 1917 it was impossible for an observer to be promoted above the rank of Lieutenant, or given any executive position, whatever qualities he might otherwise possess. Even where high level policy decisions apparently favoured an equality of treatment it was not always properly implemented. Thus, whilst the Air Council decided in 1949 to admit navigators to Cranwell, it was another seven years before a navigator actually entered the College.[4]

Such attitudes can only be explained by the perception within the Service that as the pilot takes the aircraft into action and is usually, through the technical and demanding action of flying it, the person who ensures the success of the mission, only pilots can truly appreciate the nature and demands of aerial warfare. There may be a grudging admission that navigators [or "observers" or "weapons system operators"] in multi-seat aircraft share some of demands and responsibilities, but the identification of potential high flyers has always been performed relatively early in their careers, and pilots will have been channelled directly along routes leading to the top where others will have had a more fiercely competitive struggle.

If these, sometimes formal, more often unspoken, assumptions have dominated the culture of the Service throughout its ninety year existence, then the advent of the unmanned aircraft clearly has far-reaching implications for the future Royal Air Force, implications that challenge the very nature of the Service, its self-image and the way it is perceived by the other two services and the general public. Flying is not a natural activity for man: in order to fly, he or she is entirely reliant on some form of mechanical assistance, usually of a fair degree of sophistication. Early man could and did swim and utilise logs as flotation aids, graduating to dug-out canoes and eventually sail-powered vessels. Even relatively sophisticated design ideas for achieving flight, such as those sketched out by Leonardo da Vinci, had to await developments in technology sufficient to conquer the problem of the power to weight ratio. From the very earliest days of the RFC and the RAF, flight was a dangerous activity even without the added dimension of military combat and its associated risks. Simple technical failure, all too common until fairly recently and not unknown even now [cf the recent descent of a US Airways airliner into the Hudson River in New York in January 2009 after a multiple birdstrike], was potentially fatal, and relatively straightforward misjudgements could also kill the unwary. Whilst the sea is also a potentially hostile medium, man can survive on it for short periods under his own power, or with simple buoyancy aids; it does not *automatically* kill those whose technical means of support have failed – vessels which suffer a loss of propulsive power due to mechanical failure do not automatically sink. This is not true of the air, where loss of power almost invariably removes lift and thus makes prolonged flight unsustainable, at which point, recent miraculous examples notwithstanding, survival becomes problematic, particularly for those not seated on a piece of Martin-Baker, or similar, technology.

These simple truths underpin some cultural assumptions and attitudes towards military airmen. Many people are frightened of flying even in relatively safe commercial airliners, whereas few indeed are frightened of sea voyages in ocean going ships. Such fear of flying may be exaggerated but, as the Hudson River incident shows, it is not irrational. Society has traditionally held the bravery of military men in some esteem, particularly in those previous eras when the whole of society was perceived to have benefited from their prowess. Today few in wider society are more than vaguely aware of the benefits they enjoy as the result of the sacrifice of previous generations. Although military aviation is a relatively recent phenomenon in historical terms, it might be argued that military airmen have benefited from a perception that they possess a double helping of bravery as both intrepid explorer of the "dangerous" third dimension, and as courageous combatants.

There are some very deep atavistic attitudes underlying the historical admiration of warriors and it is arguable that only in very recent times, particularly as a result of the industrialised warfare of the twentieth century, have such attitudes begun to change, at least in the West. As Christopher Coker has pointed out: "What distinguishes humans from nonhumans is that the former are not programmed to act by instinctual behaviour. They are prepared to die for honour or a flag."[5] The philosopher Hegel pointed out that war between civilized as opposed to tribal societies meant that "Warriors were now people who realized the nature of their own freedom through courage…" They were, in other words, willing to die for a value. Hegel also stated that "Freedom dies for fear of dying".[6] If we accept these strictures then we are led to the belief that there are two fundamental elements present in warfare – the instrumental and the existential. The instrumental is the rational, political element which underpins most, and certainly most Western, perceptions of war. This is the idea that any war is fought to achieve certain rational ends – in Clausewitz's famous dictum, that "War is merely the continuation of policy by other means".[7] However, this is not the only element present in war. Clausewitz himself, the arch-exponent of the rational in war, wrote "If war is an act of force, the emotions cannot fail to be involved …".[8] Hence there is also the existential element in warfare. Men and women are undoubtedly motivated to join the armed services not merely to advance the rational element, but also to experience the existential aspect – to test themselves and be tested against an idea. They subscribe, unconsciously perhaps, to an ideal that in order to be truly human, one must be tested and not found wanting, and that most people are not so tested in civil affairs. It is arguable that it is this motivation, allied to the idea of service, itself an existential concept, that drives most people who enlist in the armed forces. If the existential elements of warfare relate to concepts relating variously to bravery, self-discovery, self-image, action, vitality, adversity and trial, where does this leave the literally chair bound warrior flying a UAV, whose war is fought from a padded seat many thousand of miles away from his or her adversary?

In circumstances such as these, what is left of the concept of the serviceman or woman as being extraordinary, of bearing additional risk selflessly on behalf of others? And what of the traditionally elevated position of aircrew? If a far higher proportion of the frontline inventory is unmanned, who will fly them? At the moment, such aircraft are piloted by aircrew who have previously flown and qualified on manned aircraft. The question then becomes whether this is either desirable or sustainable in the long term. The argument in favour of aircrew is essentially that the unmanned vehicles will continue to operate in airspace with other aircraft, whether civil or military, and that an understanding and appreciation of the unusual and challenging physical environment and the effect of such factors as weather, the performance and reactions of other aircraft and pilots in a given situation and ATC procedures are crucial to their safe operation, and also to their effective military employment.

However, for the medium to long term sustainability of the Reaper unmanned aerial system [UAS] the Royal Air Force has already announced a trial involving the training of non-pilot officers as UAS pilots. The five personnel selected for the trial are to consist of two Fast Jet Weapons System Operators and three officers from the Operations Support Branch. The training will include an extensive ground-school phase "to produce a baseline of 'air mindedness' to complement the basic pilot skills." The Commanders Briefing Note announcing the trial itself indicates the degree of hesitancy, even discomfort, with which the Service has set off down this road. Hence, it contains the following prominent caveat:

> It is strongly emphasised that this activity is a trial and no decisions have been made with regard to the future policy in this area. The trail will inform any future decisions and there are no changes to extant policy regarding Branches, employment, MES or career fields, all of which will require much detailed work and AFBSC [Air Force Board Standing Committee] level approval following any emerging trial results.[9]

The long term implication may well be that the percentage of aircrew in the Service will shrink. Whilst there has always been a differential risk between those at the point of the spear and those in the shaft, and the more so in air forces for reasons alluded to at the start of this essay, what are the implications if an ever greater proportion of airmen or women are remote from risk, so that the 10 per cent of the RAF who were operationally trained aircrew in 1945 shrinks even further and the aircrew who fly unmanned vehicles bear no greater, or even lesser risk than the support personnel? What reasons for regarding them as a race apart remain, if their risk is, in fact, no different to that of the citizens in whose comfortable and unthreatened environs they continue to live, and indeed do not leave when they "go to war"? These changes are, for the Royal Air Force, amongst the most significant in cultural terms that it has ever faced, and are potentially more profound than similar challenges facing the other two services.

Furthermore, if leadership of the service is based on the ability to lead in the face of adversity and in potentially dangerous and stressful circumstances, where will the future "airman" obtain his credibility if his only experience of command, and indeed of warfare, is through an existence isolated not only from the battlefield, but from the war itself? High command remoteness is not a new phenomenon. Generals in the first World War were criticised for being remote – despite the fact that they were within a few miles of the frontline and could and did visit it, and that not a few were killed. In addition, they nearly all had some experience of warfare from earlier in their careers. Potentially, however, the UAV airman could remain remote and isolated from warfare throughout his or her career, not simply at high command level. What understanding of war as act of struggle, of its dynamic, of its complex interaction, of the spiritual dimension inherent in the concept of triumph of will, does a UAV/UCAV culture offer? Is it any more valid than a non-military actor viewing war from a comfortable chair through the medium of nightly TV news beamed to his plasma TV screen? What qualities qualify the future leaders of such a force to be leaders – the technocratic skills of the IT manager, or the leadership skills of the military man, and if it is the latter, where will they be gained? Indeed, the nature of leadership where the delivery of air power is achieved increasingly remotely will itself change and it may take a little while to establish what new qualities may be required of the leader of the future.

As we have discussed above, manned military flight has always had an element of danger, even without the malign attentions of the enemy. In part to avoid those very attentions it has been conducted at the edge of the permissible envelope, but minimising risks from the enemy increased risks from other factors, so that the inherent risks of low flying were balanced against the lessened threat from ground based air defences. The life of the airman was thus physically and mentally testing even outside war. Furthermore, although during the Second World War support personnel often bore an element of risk, especially in expeditionary operations, this was generally and reasonably considered to be less than that borne by the aircrew. Now, however, whilst the aircrew of 39 Squadron may be flying the aircraft from the reasonably assured safety of Nevada, the support personnel who oversee the launch and recovery of the aircraft are in theatre with all the attendant risks which that brings. Furthermore, there is historical evidence to suggest that the era of cold war air operations from well found main operating bases produced a culture that was in part perceptibly "unmilitary" and that this was a problem which particularly affected air forces. The new expeditionary era of Royal Air Force operations ushered in during the 1990s by operations in the Middle East and the Balkans exposed attitudes amongst some personnel which the RAF hierarchy found disturbing and which led to the adoption of the ethos of 'warfighter first, specialist second'. This was intended to reinforce the message that all personnel were in the military and subscribed to a military ethos.

However, if the existential element of warfare is reduced by its increasingly digital and robotic nature, what path does this suggest for the military ethos? What will be the ethos of cyber-warriors? They take no risk. They do not engage directly with the enemy, as nearly all previous military men have done. They are probably largely immune from retaliation. How will they be imbued with a military spirit and ethos? The heritage of their forebears in Camels, Lancasters, Vulcans or Tornado GR1s will have less resonance than the video games they played in childhood and may continue to play as adults. We may refer to their unit as No. 39 Squadron and award it the standard of its illustrious predecessors, but what meaning will it have to him or her? What, indeed, will be their ethos? If it is purely utilitarian and instrumental then their task becomes an employment, like any other. "Indeed, Hegel is quick to tell us that war cannot be centred on utilitarian motives alone, such as the defence of life or property, for this would lead to an absurd situation. It would be impossible to demand that soldiers sacrifice both their property and their lives and at the same time declare that war is waged to preserve them. If we ask why soldiers are willing to put their lives at risk, we must look at why they find it a necessary feature of their general humanity. Thus Hegel concluded that war will only come to an end when human beings no longer have need of it to express their humanity, when no one will esteem them as warriors, and thus they will no longer esteem themselves."[10]

Will there be serious issues of self-respect and motivation for such "warriors" if they come to regard it as just a job, or, conversely, will it dilute the meaning or the concept of the warrior?   There are signs that such dilution is already under way.   In a presentation to the recent RAF Centre for Air Power Studies Conference at Shrivenham Colonel Mark Wells, the Head of History at the USAF Academy at Colorado Springs has some pertinent observations on changing attitudes within the USAF.[11]   Colonel Wells, himself a qualified KC-135 pilot, referred to a recent incident in which one of the young military officers serving on the teaching staff in his department had told him that he was a veteran of "combat" who had seen service in four wars.   Since he knew the officer involved to be a relatively junior intelligence specialist, Colonel Wells asked him to elucidate.   All of the examples of "combat" cited by the officer actually involved deployments which, in Wells's words, were "several hundred miles from actual combat", such as a deployment in Italy during the Kosovo campaign.   The officer was surprised and upset when he was told that such deployments did not count as "combat" in Wells's lexicon.   Colonel Wells's definition of a combatant was that of a fighter, a warrior if you will, but one who definitely fights.   He understood "Air combat … to be the use of military aircraft and other flying machines in warfare or the close-range aerial combat between military aircraft themselves.   Centuries of warfare and military history strongly suggest that being in combat actually puts a combatant at some personal risk."   This was the traditional view with which Colonel Wells found himself in sympathy, but he also quoted the following words from the *US Air Force Officers' Guide*, which he described as a quasi-official guide for newly qualified USAF officers:

> Combat is too often described as being only the event of deadly encounters between two adversaries. Not so. Combat is more [sic] often the tiresome struggles to supply aviation material, such as fuel, at the proper time and place in the combat zone. Combat is frequently the effort to produce sanitary water and potable food in an area where it is almost impossible to do so … to furnish needed parts for inoperable aircraft … to operate a decent eating facility in indecent … combat is doing the best you can under the circumstances

Colonel Wells also identified other elements which had traditionally been the preserve of "warrior" aircrew and which were now suffering similar dilution. He highlighted uniform, or perhaps more accurately clothing, as one example, saying that "Not too many years ago, for example, flying gear and flight suits were the sole domain of aviators.   Occupying as they did the status of warriors in the Air Force, these aircrew members went to some lengths to distinguish themselves from non-flyers".   He suggested that it might be argued that many recent changes which have seen non-aircrew increasingly wearing flight suits "have come as a deliberate attempt to further narrow the distinction between traditional warriors … and the other members of the service." He also pointed to the existence of sub-cultures among aviators – a phenomenon also prevalent in the RAF, with its various sub-tribes of "mud-movers", "truckies" and "the kipper fleet".

Wells also quoted a recent USAF Chief of Staff as stating that being a "warrior" was more "a state of mind" than actual experience. If combat in future is accepted as merely doing ones best under difficult circumstances then the range of combat "veterans" will increase exponentially. Whilst conceding that neither view would necessarily meet with universal acceptance in the USAF, they indicate the extent to which traditional views of warfare and warriors, forged quite literally over millennia, are being challenged. Such trends are by no means limited to the USAF. The RAF is increasingly inclined to allocate squadron numberplates, previously ferociously defended as the preserve of *frontline* flying squadrons, to units who have no frontline combat task in either peace or war. Similarly, during the deliberations over the award of RAF Battle Honours in the wake of the Kosovo conflict, with which the author was intimately involved, some senior officers questioned whether the regulations on the award of Battle Honours contained in AP3327 were too restrictive. In particular they questioned whether the regulations governing the right to "emblazon" an Honour on the standard were outdated in requiring that this accolade be limited to squadrons which had been in direct confrontation with the enemy and had demonstrated gallantry and spirit "under fire".[12]   It was suggested to the Battle Honours Committee that this approach no longer took account of the realities of modern air warfare, in that modern, ground-based air defence systems posed a potential threat to aircraft at very long range and that the term "under fire" therefore had little meaning. Thus a *potential* threat to the operators was equated with the *actual* threat and by extension with combat itself, using Colonel Wells's definition. It seems reasonable to conclude that these already very perceptible cultural shifts within Air Forces will potentially be highlighted and accelerated by the increasing prevalence of unmanned systems. In this respect the allocation of the 39 Squadron numberplate to a unit flying unmanned vehicles should surely be seen as a significant pointer for the future.

Yet comparatively speaking "combat" for modern ground forces can still be a dangerous pursuit and the existential element is very much present, as the casualty figures from Afghanistan demonstrate only too clearly. This may increase the cultural gap which has developed in recent years between airmen and soldiers. Interestingly, for the RAF (excepting the RAF Regiment) it has been helicopter and air transport aircraft which have been most exposed in recent conflicts and which have suffered losses to hostile causes. There is little doubt that the crews of these aircraft are warriors engaged in combat.

To be humanistic, war and warriors must respect the enemy; not necessarily their ideas or methods, but their humanity. Yet respect requires personal engagement at some level. War has historically been an intersubjective activity. "War [has] involved a dialogue with the adversary on the intersubjective plane."[13] The language of the dialogue is of course violence. This raises the question of whether unmanned vehicles, whose operators can only experience war through a datalink, are in any meaningful sense involved in a "dialogue" with their adversary. Does the UAVs inherent lack of personal engagement encourage a lack of respect for one's enemy and through that, a dangerous degree of detachment?   Nietzsche identified this conundrum when he wrote "You may have only enemies you can hate not enemies you despise. You must be proud of your enemy: then the successes of your enemy are your success also".[14]

Are UAVs the *reductio ad absurdum* of the Western obsession with technology? Speaking of the Romans, Josiah Ober described the siege of Jerusalem, which included endless and senseless killing as personifying "the long, complex, ugly western tradition of war … as a technological problem".[15] In UAVs, have we reached a point where we have become so smart technologically that we are unable to see concomitant conceptual and philosophical dangers inherent in them?   Rather than a *Deus ex machina* are the machine and its operator becoming *Deus in machina*? If war really does become a system, systematized in the way UAVs suggest, is it war?   And if war is unilaterally depersonalized and dehumanised to that extent, what does that speak to in the society or service that wages it?   The Roman Empire collapsed when the Roman citizen was no longer required to defend it as part of its own legions, which were instead sub-contracted out to the German tribes. If western society views the military as something apart, and with some suspicion because of the increasing perception that military activity is itself unworthy, how will it view 'airmen' whose military activity involves taking little or no personal risks; what 'military covenant' or respect will there be for a technocrat who 'fights' such wars?

Additionally, if UAV crews are entirely divorced from the reality and the context of what they are doing, if they perceive no difference between their actions and those in a computer game or simulation, what effects will this have? Will it make warfare increasingly and literally "inhuman", so that by removing the possibility of friendly casualties, an act which can be perceived on one level as "humane" (though it can also be perceived simultaneously as politically shrewd in a casualty averse society), it will remove necessary and age old restraints? If war for the airman, and the concomitant killing, becomes "just a job", with no risk, and no reward in terms of self-knowledge, what effects will that have, both on how it is waged and on those who wage it?   To remove man from the equation as UAVs do is in one sense to allow war to become in a quite literal way inhuman, with potentially profound consequences. Furthermore, with no context and no reality what perception of possible disadvantage in terms of the effects of the action can the operator have?   There are innumerable instances in history of the exercise of restraint in military situations because the physical presence of the operator has allowed him to exercise his wider human understanding of context to perceive the military advantage of foregoing or limiting the application of force.

It might be argued that Rules Of Engagement provides some insurance against this tendency, but ROE can only provide guidance as to when it is **permissible** to engage a target, they cannot provide assurance that it is the correct action to take in a given situation. The distinguished military historian John Terraine has pointed out that the aircrews of Bomber Command during the Second World War went cheerfully about their business of raining death and destruction on civilians in the cities of Germany, but that in all probability they were only capable of doing so because the physical separation from the effects of their efforts produced a similar distancing in psychological terms.[16] This is not the place to debate the morality of the strategic bomber offensive, although this author is firmly of the opinion that it was a necessary evil. However, there can be no doubt that the young aircrews of Bomber Command most certainly put their own life and limb on the line in the cause of duty, and that they paid a consistently high price in terms of casualties. Whilst they may have been distanced from the results of their bombs, they were all too uncomfortably close to the considerable efforts of their enemies to similarly immolate them or blast them into oblivion. In that sense they were definitely warriors, but it is difficult to argue that UCAV crews merit the same accolade. And as the latter's physical and thus psychological distancing is even greater, it is legitimate to ask what effects it might have on the waging of war.

Although in the short to medium term the manned aircraft will still form the core of the RAF's inventory, in the long term the UAV may come to predominate. The questions posed here about the inherent cultural structure and attitudes of the Service, which are only just beginning to impinge on traditional attitudes, will then come sharply into focus. Indeed, the question which lurks unasked in the background is surely the most fundamental one of all. In the era of unmanned predominance "What need of a separate air force?"

By its nature this essay has raised many questions and provided few if any answers: but to do so was not its intention. Instead it is intended to stimulate debate about the impact of unmanned aerial systems on the ethos and military culture of the Royal Air Force.

NOTES

[1] Dave English, *Slipping The Surly Bonds – Great Quotations on Flight* (McGraw-Hill, NY, 1998) p.2
[2] English, p.129
[3] All statistics in this and the following paragraph taken from *Royal Air Force Personnel Statistics for the period 3 September 1939 to 1 September 1945.*
[4] C G Jefford, *Observers and Navigators* (Shrewsbury, 2001) pp. 51 & 223. This work charts in some detail the history of navigators in the RFC and RAF and gives further insights into the supremacy of the pilot-oriented culture of the Service.
[5] Christopher Coker, *Waging War Without Warriors? The changing culture of military conflict* (Lyne Reiner, Colorado 2002) p.55.
[6] Quoted in Coker p.55.
[7] Carl von Clausewitz, *On War*, edited and translated by Michael Howard and

Peter Paret, (Princeton 1989) p.87.

[8] On War p.76.

[9] RAF Commanders' Briefing Note 020/09 "Trial to select and train non-pilot junior officers to meet Reaper Operational Conversion Course entry standard", 17 February 2009.

[10] Quoted in Coker pp.54-55.

[11] All quotations are from Colonel Mark Wells, *Calling Ourselves Warriors: Dodging a Bullet and Becoming a Hero*, paper presented to the RAF Centre for Air Power Studies/Kings College Conference on Air Power and Strategy, Joint Services Command & Staff College, 12-13 June 2008. I am grateful to Colonel Wells for providing me with a copy of his paper.

[12] D/AHB(RAF)3/2.

[13] Coker p.37.

[14] Nietzsche 'Thus Spake Zarathustra' – quoted in Coker p.38.

[15] Quoted in Coker p.58.

[16] John Terraine, *The Right of the Line: The Royal Air Force in the European War 1939-1945*, (London, 1985) p.512.

THE STRATEGIC IMPACT OF UNMANNED
AERIAL VEHICLES

Prof Philip Sabin

Unmanned air vehicles (UAVs) have for decades been making a small but growing contribution to the panoply of aerospace power in general (especially in the Western world), and this contribution is set to increase further in the decades to come as the computing power on which UAV capabilities are based continues to improve. This chapter takes a broad look at the phenomenon, and asks what (if any) difference the essentially tactical innovation of a diminished need for human crews in aircraft themselves makes to the characteristics of aerospace power at the strategic level.

The chapter begins by reviewing the distinctive attributes of aerospace power as a whole, and how these have developed by the early 21st century, a hundred years after powered flight was first achieved. It goes on to analyse the strategic impact of UAVs in terms of two offsetting dimensions – first their potential benefits compared to other forms of aerospace power, and then their potential problems in the same context. The chapter concludes by addressing several fundamental issues, namely whether the advent of UAVs is more of an evolution or revolution in aerospace power, whether their relationship with other air and space systems is more one of competition or complementarity, what impact the growing use of UAVs will have on the presently overwhelming US aerospace dominance, and finally how it will affect traditional service specialisations.

Aerospace Power in General

A clear trend in military doctrine has been towards an inclusive and maximalist perspective on the various components of air and space power. Hence, Britain defines 'air power' as 'The ability to project military force in air or space by or from a platform or missile operating above the surface of the earth', and it goes on to explain that 'Air platforms are defined as any aircraft, helicopter or unmanned air vehicle'.[1] This maximalist perspective has three important consequences – that air and space are usually treated as part of a continuum despite the different physical properties of the atmospheric and orbital environments, that air power is spread across all services rather than being limited to traditional air forces, and that UAVs are already firmly encompassed within the existing doctrinal framework.

There have been many attempts to identify the distinguishing characteristics of aerospace power, and these efforts are often heavily influenced by advocacy or 'political correctness'. British Air Power Doctrine, for instance, lists no fewer than 17 defining characteristics, putting them in alphabetical rather than priority order, and including such elements as 'Aircraft Carriers' and 'Coalition Capability'.[2] For our purposes, it is probably better to go back to basics and to focus on what really distinguishes aerospace from surface power, so as to identify the fundamentals on which other so-called 'defining characteristics' are built. I would argue that there are three such fundamental strengths of aerospace power, which are as follows:

Perspective

From the earliest days of balloons, the height which flight makes possible has granted a perspective much less constrained by terrain and limited surface horizons (though inhibited by vegetation and cloud cover), allowing direct lines of sight over a very wide area at the cost of increased distance from the ground. In the ultimate case, a geosynchronous satellite can observe over a third of the Earth's surface from 36,000 km up.

Speed

The lower frictional resistance of the air allows air vehicles to attain speeds around an order of magnitude higher than their land or naval counterparts. In space, the virtual absence of atmospheric resistance allows speeds of well over an order of magnitude higher still (28,000 km per hour for satellites in low Earth orbit).[3]

Overflight

Height also frees air and space vehicles from the constraints which surface vehicles face by being limited to either the land or sea environments and (on land) of being further constrained by multiple terrain obstacles and often dependent on specific linear routes. Aerospace platforms can move freely in three dimensions regardless of geography, making it all but impossible to block their progress at specific 'choke points'.

It is from these three fundamental physical attributes that other aerospace power characteristics flow. 'Reach' and 'Penetration', for instance, stem from the combination of Speed and Overflight, allowing air vehicles to avoid defences and strike quickly against targets deep in enemy territory, even though they may actually possess less absolute range and endurance than (say) a nuclear attack submarine. Indeed, there is one further physical attribute which is a fundamental limitation of aerospace power, as follows:

Energy Needs

Overcoming gravity without resting on land or water requires large energy expenditure per unit of payload, either constantly (to maintain the necessary airflow over wings or rotor blades) or in the initial surge (to give ballistic missiles or satellites the enormous height and speed required for sub-orbital or orbital flight). Since the fuel needed to provide the energy is itself heavy, a vicious circle of escalating energy needs is created.

From this fundamental limitation flow several other oft-cited characteristics of aerospace power. 'Impermanence' and 'Base Dependence' reflect the need of air vehicles to return to base more frequently than deployed surface forces to refuel and rearm, as well as the inability of satellites in their ballistic trajectory to loiter over a single point except through the unique circumstance of a distant geostationary orbit. 'Fragility' and 'Payload Cost' reflect how energy needs increase sharply with vehicle weight, and hence how difficult it is for air or space platforms to carry thick armour or very heavy loads as surface vehicles often do.

'Flexibility' is frequently claimed as a key attribute of aerospace power, and it is certainly true that their distinctive Speed allows air vehicles to be re-tasked quickly across a wide battle area. However, it is hard to argue that an aircraft is inherently any *more* flexible and versatile than a surface warship or an infantry battalion, given the ability of these latter to interact sensitively with the local environment across the spectrum from peace to war. Satellites, with their very limited ability to change their trajectory and role once deployed into orbit, seem even less deserving of the claim that they are any more flexible than other forms of military power. This does not mean that aerospace forces are not flexible, just that they are not uniquely so.

Whereas the above characteristics have applied throughout the entire history of aerospace power, some other features have become especially prominent over the past two decades. I would identify two main areas of growing aerospace strength, and two offsetting areas of growing aerospace problems. The strengths are as follows:

Precision

As demonstrated above all in the 1991 Gulf War, the advent of precision guidance has increased by orders of magnitude the potential accuracy of air-delivered munitions, and so has made target identification rather than payload limitations the key constraint on the dominance of aerial firepower.[4]   Precision surveillance capabilities have improved commensurately, overcoming some of the trade-off between range and breadth of vision, and allowing aerospace platforms to focus on a chosen area in fine detail even from great heights.

Network Integration

Increasingly effective networking has become the dominant characteristic of both air and surface forces in the modern era, but the aerospace contribution has become even more important thanks to this ever-growing exchange of data in real time. Not only is the Perspective which aircraft and satellites provide more useful than ever when it is transmitted immediately to other forces, but satellite based positioning systems are becoming increasingly vital for navigation and weapon guidance, and aircraft are able to use their

Speed to approach and engage fleeting targets as soon as they are observed by other air or surface forces.[5]

The two offsetting problems for modern air power are as follows:

Cost

Air power has always been costly due to its position at the leading edge of technology, but the continuing offence-defence race has combined with the end of the Cold War to produce a situation in which programmes for new manned combat aircraft such as Eurofighter or the F-22 drag on for decades of uncertainty as countries try to come to grips with the enormous costs involved.[6] Military space capabilities are just as expensive, and even such a leading air power as the UK has a very limited panoply of satellites.[7]

Casualty Sensitivity

Whereas aerial attrition in the era of the World Wars reached terrifying proportions, the combination of less than vital interests and media amplification of the slightest loss has made air arms even more sensitive than surface forces to taking casualties in modern campaigns, as illustrated by the shooting down and subsequent rescue of Scott O'Grady in Bosnia in 1995.[8] Not only that, but (as recent experience in Afghanistan and Pakistan demonstrates all too clearly) unintended 'collateral damage' from air attack has for similar reasons become equally problematic, unlike in the World Wars when the prospect of civilian casualties did not inhibit the wholesale bombing even of friendly cities under enemy occupation.[9]

The current prevalence of 'asymmetric warfare' rather than the more symmetrical confrontations of the World War and Cold War eras thus has distinctly double-edged consequences for aerospace power.[10] On the one hand, technological and political trends have combined to give Western (especially US) aerospace capabilities virtually unchallenged dominance in any conflict, without the bloody and drawn-out attritional air contests of previous eras.[11] On the other hand, the growing pervasiveness of what Rupert Smith has termed 'Wars among the People' has forced Western air power into a reactive and constabulary mode in which (as in the continuing operations in Iraq and Afghanistan) less than 1% of sorties involve the actual dropping of ordnance.[12] Even in more intensive air campaigns like those in Kosovo in 1999 or Lebanon in 2006, able adversaries have been able to conceal their fielded forces in tangled terrain and employ political countermeasures so as to make it far harder than expected for the superior air power to prevail.[13]

Having outlined the advantages and problems of aerospace power in general in the early 21st century, it is now time to focus in on the growing contribution of UAVs, starting with the strengths they may bring to military capability at the strategic level.

Potential Benefits of UAVs

To my mind, the main strategic advantages of UAVs fall into three broad categories – Cost-Effectiveness, Pervasiveness, and Casualty Avoidance. I will discuss each of these areas in turn.

Cost-Effectiveness US spending on UAVs currently stands at over $2 bn per year.[14] This is a lot of money, but it is only around one-tenth of what the US spends on military space capabilities, and less than half a percent of US defence spending as a whole.[15] The real question concerns the efficiency of the investment in generating military capability, compared to alternative uses of the resources concerned. This is a hard question to answer because of the complexity of the comparative process, but two useful observations may be made.

First, there is a clear trade-off between cost and capability across the very wide range of UAV types, from hand-launched tactical vehicles like Dragon Eye, costing only tens of thousands of dollars each, all the way to sophisticated strategic platforms such as Global Hawk which cost tens of millions of dollars per copy, a similar price to that of manned fighter aircraft.[16] With no simple metric to compare the diverse contributions of UAVs across this enormous cost and capability range, and with only the high end of the range being easily comparable to the alternative capabilities provided by manned aircraft or satellites, the difficulty of measuring cost-effectiveness becomes apparent.

Second, one must examine the through-life costs of entire UAV systems, rather than focusing too narrowly on the airframes themselves. Doing without on-board crew obviously yields significant savings in loaded weight thanks to the absence of cockpits, but overall manning requirements are likely to be unaffected given the support and maintenance burden and given the need for remote operators who may have to use a shift system to sustain the increased endurance of the vehicles. Similarly, lower platform acquisition costs may be offset by higher loss rates through accidents and enemy action.[17] Considerations such as these have led some observers to suggest that, from an overall perspective, the apparent financial advantages of UAVs may prove illusory.[18]

On the other hand, the continuing prominence of UAVs such as Predator (costing a few million dollars each) in the campaigns in Iraq and Afghanistan suggests a highly worthwhile return on the relatively modest current investment. The sheer number of UAV development programmes, and the speed with which innovations such as Predator B (Reaper) have been brought into service, stand in stark contrast to the paucity and inertia of current manned combat aircraft programmes, especially after the onset of the global financial crisis.[19] UAV technology is still in its infancy compared to more traditional aerospace systems, and future developments seem likely to mitigate such current problems as high mishap rates and intensive demands for skilled operators.[20]   Although one should certainly not exaggerate the cost-effectiveness benefits of UAVs compared to manned aircraft or satellites, UAVs do seem to offer at least a partial answer to the endemic aerospace problems of cost escalation which I discussed earlier.

Pervasiveness   I have already mentioned the enormous range of capability offered by different UAVs, and this diversity is in itself a major strategic benefit. Manned vehicles have to be above a certain minimum size and weight if they are to accommodate their crew, and their endurance (even with in-flight refuelling) is limited by that of the humans on board. Although some UAVs are essentially just like crewless versions of manned platforms (literally so in the case of the conversions of existing airframes which have taken place sporadically since before World War Two), most UAVs exploit their liberation from the constraints of human presence to 'push the envelope' of capability in various strategically significant ways.[21]

One approach which has already become well established is to create smaller and lighter airframes than manned vehicles would allow. Almost all UAVs weigh considerably less than the 10,000 kg or so of modern fighter jets, and although some such as Predator at around 1,000 kg are similar in weight to light utility aircraft or scout helicopters, others are much lighter still, down to just 2 kg for the US Raven and Dragon Eye systems.[22]   This has two important consequences. First, even the relatively limited current spending on UAVs has already allowed NATO to field around 6,700 operational airframes (all but 500 or so being small, tactical vehicles).[23]   Second, the small UAVs can be launched, operated and recovered by deployed surface forces, giving even tiny detachments their own organic access to the elevated Perspective which has always been one of the core benefits of air power. Continuing advances in miniaturisation are prompting the development of still smaller 'micro air vehicles' weighing only 0.2 kg, though more radical predictions of insect-sized UAVs snooping covertly on enemy buildings seem to be some way from realisation.[24]

A second approach which capitalises on freedom from the constraints (and weight) of a human crew is to increase the flight endurance of UAVs. The categorisation of larger UAVs as either MALE (Medium Altitude Long Endurance) or HALE (High Altitude Long Endurance) already emphasises this aspect, and maximum flight times of 20-30 hours are typical.[25]   Although manned heavy bombers have matched such flight times on an exceptional basis during intercontinental missions using multiple in-flight refuelling, UAVs employ such endurance routinely to offset their usually slow transit speeds (around 100 knots for Predator A and 200 knots for Predator B) and to increase their persistence in the combat area well beyond that of manned platforms. Increased endurance and satellite control relays also allow UAVs to operate at extended range, as in the recent Israeli strike on an arms convoy in Sudan.[26] There are schemes to use high altitude airships to boost UAV endurance by a further order of magnitude or even more, and projects such as Britain's Zephyr programme make true capital out of the absence of human crew by employing solar cells and storage batteries to overcome completely the vicious circle of fuel dependence and to keep an ultra-light airframe aloft for projected missions of months at a time.[27]

The net strategic impact of this pushing of the envelope of capability is that UAVs increase the pervasiveness of aerospace power by making it more likely that hostile activity will be observed from above. Just as the proliferation of CCTV cameras has made it virtually impossible for citizens in developed countries to avoid being caught repeatedly on camera, so the proliferation of smaller (so more numerous) and larger (so more persistent) UAVs makes it harder for surface combatants to expose themselves outside buildings or forests without the risk of detection.[28] Whereas manned aircraft are constrained by limited fuel and by the safety of their crew, and satellites have no choice but to flash across the sky in their predictable orbital trajectory, UAVs can afford to loiter and stare and even to move in closer to investigate and track suspect movements. This is why UAVs have come into their own during the continuing conflicts against elusive insurgents in Iraq and Afghanistan, and the process seems likely to continue (at least in similar conflicts) in years to come.

Casualty Avoidance I mentioned earlier the increased sensitivity of Western nations to the loss of aircraft in modern campaigns. This is in large part a product of these nations' very success in avoiding the fearful aerial attrition of earlier eras, thanks to the technological dominance which Western air power now enjoys. Hence, when a single F-117 was shot down during Operation Allied Force in 1999, it provided a significant propaganda boost to the Serbs, even though the pilot was rescued.[29] Fear of losing aircrew (and especially of having them taken hostage) contributed to the non-employment of the Apache helicopters of Task Force Hawk during the Kosovo campaign, and also to the controversial (though often misrepresented) reluctance to send jets into the anti-aircraft danger zone below 15,000 ft.[30]

UAVs have demonstrably provided a way around this sensitivity about air losses, since they have been placed much more at risk than manned platforms have been in recent campaigns, and their loss in combat has not produced anything like the media interest or propaganda value associated with the shooting down of manned aircraft. The US used (and often lost) many UAVs over communist territory during the Cold War, with nothing of the embarrassment associated with the capture of U-2 pilot Gary Powers in central Russia in 1960. UAVs continue to be especially suited for such politically delicate missions, as in their current extensive utilisation by the CIA to target al-Qaeda and Taleban militants in Pakistan.[31] In 1999, 45 UAVs of all types were lost to enemy action and technical failure during the 78 days of Operation Allied Force, but this fact was hardly noticed compared to the remarkable achievement of not losing a single member of NATO aircrew in combat.[32] UAVs have even been sent on suicidal missions to draw enemy fire, as with the two Predators sent over Baghdad on the first day of Operation Iraqi Freedom, when the main reaction of commentators was to ridicule the Iraqis for failing to shoot them down and then for trying to find the non-existent pilots when the Predators ditched for lack of fuel.[33] There could be no clearer contrast with the added costs and risks of combat search and rescue missions if manned aircraft are downed.[34]

Not only do UAVs remove the risk of aircrew casualties during their own missions, but their contribution can also help to protect other friendly air and surface forces during the campaign as a whole. Israel's use of Scout UAVs to provoke and pinpoint Syrian SAMs in the Bekaa valley in 1982 famously helped them to destroy around 20 SAM batteries for the loss of only a few manned aircraft during the campaign, in stark contrast to the 1973 war when several dozen Israeli jets were lost to the formidable Arab air defences.[35] As regards surface forces, although the US alone has suffered around 4,000 fatalities during the continuing conflicts in Iraq and Afghanistan, these losses would surely have been higher still if it were not for the surveillance and warning provided by UAVs – in November 2007, General James Simmons in Baghdad described these systems as a 'decisive factor' in the dramatic recent drop in attacks by improvised explosive devices.[36] All in all, the reduction of friendly casualties must be accounted a significant strategic benefit of the increasing contribution made by UAVs to modern campaigns.

Potential Problems of UAVs

UAVs have several strategic disadvantages to set against these positive aspects, and I would highlight in particular the 'Revolution of Rising Expectations' which they may fuel, the Limitations of Unmanned Systems compared to those with human crews, and the risk of Adversary Employment of UAVs themselves. Again, I will discuss each of these dimensions in turn.

Revolution of Rising Expectations   Any improvement in human conditions tends very quickly to be taken for granted and established as the new norm, with any slippage or reversal being seen as a serious crisis. This explains the changing absolute definitions of poverty, and the preoccupation with ever more remote health and safety risks (such as 'mad cow' disease or child abduction) as earlier more common dangers are overcome. In exactly the same way, the strategic benefits which UAVs bring may be taken for granted in ways which actually undermine the benefits themselves.

One way in which this may occur is through reinforcement of casualty sensitivity. UAVs have played a significant role in the sharp reduction in Western aircrew losses over the past three decades compared to earlier experience during the Vietnam and Yom Kippur wars, but zero aerial casualties has now become very much the norm and expectation, so there may be little choice but to employ UAVs more and more while using manned platforms with great caution to avoid any resurgence of risk as air defences become more capable in the future.[37] Whenever ground forces suffer casualties, politicians, journalists and bereaved relatives now routinely demand better protective measures such as body armour, on the grounds that everything possible should be done to protect 'our boys' (and girls).[38]   A British Army recruitment video shown hundreds of times on UK television in recent years focuses squarely on the contribution of tactical UAVs in keeping foot patrols safer, so it is hardly surprising if such overhead protection becomes seen as the norm, and its absence a matter of criminal negligence.

It is already the case that ground convoys in Iraq and Afghanistan are reluctant to deploy without UAV support, and this risks creating an over-dependence which may make Coalition actions more constrained and predictable, and which could even be exploited through deliberate distraction of the UAV's narrow focus by a spoof threat while the real attack comes from elsewhere.[39] The networked distribution of compelling real-time UAV video is also encouraging even distant senior commanders to look over their subordinates' shoulders and to micro-manage tactical engagements (or to postpone them until the video feed is available), so much so that such live video has been termed 'Predator porn' or 'CAOC crack'.[40]

It is all very well saying that officers at all levels should be more robust and flexible and more willing to delegate and take risks, but the point is that the UAV genie is already out of the bottle, and cannot simply be ignored. Just as the availability of precision-guided munitions has in itself made Western nations much more sensitive to collateral damage now that it is actually practical to minimise it in a way that it never was before, so UAVs bring with them not just capabilities but also responsibilities which shape the way in which war is conducted. The Revolution of Rising Expectations is a real and powerful phenomenon, as is clearly illustrated by the traumatic nature of the air campaigns in Kosovo in 1999 and Lebanon in 2006 despite significantly lower levels of friendly losses and civilian casualties than in many previous wars.[41]   Like most military advances, UAVs will have some of their positive contribution offset by the need to run harder just to stay in the same place.

Limitations of Unmanned Systems   Just as computers can do some calculations far better than humans but have nowhere near the all-round competence of the super-intelligent androids of science fiction, so UAVs have some serious limitations compared to manned aircraft, to set against their advantages in areas like weight and endurance. Although UAV cameras can zoom in and handle multi-spectral imagery, it is hard for them to mimic the human eye's wonderful combination of central acuity and wide peripheral vision.[42]   An even more important and intractable limitation on UAVs today lies in the very restricted capacity of artificial intelligence to think and process information as does the human brain.

The current response to this problem is to retain an off-board human crew and to exploit network integration to download sensory inputs from the UAV and upload flight commands in real time (even at intercontinental distances). However, this 'remote control' approach has serious weaknesses besides the high manning and operating costs which I have already mentioned. The communications links and relay platforms are vulnerable to mishap or to interference by a sophisticated opponent, either of which could cause loss of the vehicle (and in the worst case of the entire fleet). Downloading a continuing flood of raw video data also uses up massive communications bandwidth – so much so that a single Global Hawk consumes 5 times as much bandwidth as all the US forces engaged in Operation Enduring Freedom in 2001![43]   Although the bandwidth available has also been expanding by successive orders of magnitude in order to cope with such massive data flows, this expansion now seems to be reaching its limits, so the pure 'remote control' approach is clearly not ideal for the future development of UAVs.[44]

Much current effort is being devoted to giving future UAVs more autonomy, so as to reduce the exhausting and manpower-intensive need for remote piloting, and to allow the vehicles themselves to analyse and act on at least some of the data they receive, rather than handing it all off mindlessly and in such a bandwidth-intensive fashion for interpretation elsewhere. The extreme possibility of entirely independent vehicles which make their own automatic decisions on where to fly and what to attack seems unlikely to be realised in the foreseeable future, since it raises all sorts of legal and political problems as discussed elsewhere in this volume, and since it goes against the whole trend of network integration within modern armed forces as a whole. However, an intermediate level of autonomy which allows UAVs to make their own way between selected waypoints and to sort the wheat from the chaff in the data they receive would greatly ease the remote manning and bandwidth burden and would reduce the risk of vehicle loss if communications links were disrupted. This level of autonomy seems perfectly achievable in due course, and should allow the development of an optimal balance between artificial intelligence and human insight and direction.[45]

Experience to date has found UAV mishap rates to be at least 10 times higher than for manned military aircraft. This is a serious concern, since military jets themselves are around 100 times less safe than commercial airliners – by 2005, the US had lost only 6 F-16s in combat but nearly 300 in accidents. However, the UAV accident rate has been declining sharply over time as more experience has been gained with these vehicles, and this decline seems likely to continue.[46]   A key need is for a 'sense and avoid' capability to stop UAVs crashing blindly into other aircraft in increasingly crowded airspace, due to the very limited field of vision of their sensors. This is just one of the many technical and procedural improvements which will be needed if UAVs are to be accepted as safe for flight in ordinary civilian airspace, as manned military aircraft already are.[47]

Of even greater importance from a strategic perspective is the vulnerability of UAVs to enemy air defences. Existing models benefit from their small size and limited radar cross section, but suffer from their low speed and lack of threat awareness. 18 Pioneer UAVs were shot down during Operation Desert Storm, and 26 UAVs of various types were downed during Operation Allied Force, not counting those destroyed in accidents.[48]   UAV combat losses in Afghanistan and Iraq started out at only around 2 per year, but in 2007 several Predators were lost, and in 2008 Georgia had several UAVs shot down over Abkhazia in the run-up to the war with Russia.[49] More sophisticated air defences clearly pose the greatest threat, and there is a very difficult trade-off between giving UAVs the kind of survivability features possessed by manned aircraft (speed, countermeasures and stealth) and maintaining the lightness and cheapness which make UAVs so attractive (and relatively expendable) in the first place.

Adversary Employment   Historically, unmanned aircraft and missiles have been the weapons of the weak at least as much as the strong, since they have offered a way of striking back against a superior air power without losing scarce skilled pilots or relying on vulnerable airfields. Nazi Germany's V-1s and V-2s, Iraq's modified Scud missiles and the rockets of Hizbollah and Hamas all fit into this pattern of unmanned long range bombardment systems which can be fired from concealed or mobile launchers as an indiscriminate response to enemy dominance in the air.[50] When inferior air powers have desired greater terminal accuracy, they have tended to use not unmanned systems but highly committed and self-sacrificial human volunteer aircrew, as with the Japanese Kamikazes and the September 11th hijackers, and as with the raids by light aircraft belonging to the beleaguered Tamil Tigers more recently.[51]

There have been a few instances in recent years of UAVs proper being used against Western nations, as with the filming by the Iranians of a US carrier in the Persian Gulf and the sporadic overflights of northern Israel by Hizbollah UAVs.[52] Downed Western UAVs may even be captured and reverse engineered by more sophisticated adversaries, as China did when it copied US Firebee systems which crashed or were shot down while on covert spying missions during the Vietnam war.[53] However, it seems unlikely that inferior air powers will seek to use UAVs for anything like the continuous and closely networked real time surveillance which the West has pioneered. Although it would not be easy for Western powers to intercept small and elusive enemy UAVs or to jam their encrypted line of sight communications, the task should not be impossible if the adversary really does try to fight a fully-fledged two-sided network war. The most that the majority of enemies could reasonably expect is to get a few uncoordinated glimpses of the battle area, and the added value this would provide is questionable given that fixed sites can already be examined at leisure using freely downloadable satellite imagery.

The one role in which UAV-type technology does pose a very serious threat in the hands of inferior air powers is that for which they have already employed other unmanned systems on many occasions in the past, namely one-way retaliatory strikes. It is surprising that such antagonists have not yet made much use of modern cruise missile technology, since it offers greater terminal accuracy than rockets or Scud-derivatives, as well as the ability to evade the burgeoning threat of ballistic missile defences.[54] UAVs employ much the same airframe, propulsion and guidance technology as cruise missiles,and perhaps the biggest risk of their continued proliferation is that this will finally tempt 'underdogs' to include an air-breathing element within their asymmetric retaliatory means. While Western experts preoccupy themselves with the ethical and legal questions surrounding the possible incorporation of fully autonomous UAVs into their own arsenals, the real problem may lie in the threatened acquisition of 'kamikaze' UAVs by their adversaries, especially in the context of continuing concern about the linkage with non-conventional payloads.

Conclusion

Now that I have outlined the principal strategic benefits and problems which UAVs bring to the existing panoply of aerospace forces, I will close by addressing several key summary issues.

Evolution or Revolution? Commentators are fond of discussing weapons advances in terms of successive 'revolutions in military affairs'.[55] UAVs certainly contain some revolutionary elements, in particular their increasing miniaturisation and extended endurance, but it is hard to argue that they themselves truly revolutionise aerospace power. They have been around for decades in various forms, and are still only at the periphery in terms of funding compared to other platforms like satellites and manned aircraft. In some ways their contribution is less to introduce new ways of war than to turn the clock back to the early years of the twentieth century, when large numbers of light aircraft based in fields near the front line ranged the skies looking for targets below, before cost escalation and casualty sensitivity concentrated manned air power into much smaller numbers of higher value platforms.

That being said, modern UAVs are actually creatures of a very different strategic context, and make sense only in the world of network integration when it is feasible to go sniper-hunting over Baghdad from an air-conditioned office outside Las Vegas.[56] Whereas the biplanes of World War One lent themselves to the symmetrical attritional bloodbaths of industrial conflict, UAVs today form part of a fundamentally asymmetric strategic situation characterised by one dominant antagonist using its web of networked assets to pinpoint and strike precisely at technologically inferior opponents who have fewer scruples and greater individual commitment, and who respond with concealment, decentralisation and a hit and run approach. Although UAVs themselves may not be entirely revolutionary, the networked and computerised global military system which has given rise to them in their modern form certainly is.

Competition or Complementarity? The standard view which airmen usually espouse about UAVs is that they perform an increasingly useful complementary role, carrying out the 'dirty, dull and dangerous' missions without undermining the continuing mainstream need for manned aircraft and satellites.[57] This stance has a great deal of logic, since UAVs have indeed historically been most useful in roles such as reconnaissance and the suppression of enemy air defences, where their limited payload capacity has been least problematic and their low cost and lack of vulnerable crew has allowed bolder overflight of enemy positions. The proliferation of tiny tactical UAVs provides a new add-on capability without impinging on an existing aerospace role. The direct arming of Predators with light weapons made available by the precision revolution does tread more on the toes of manned combat aircraft, but as soon as one starts to create true unmanned combat air vehicles (UCAVs) with enhanced speed, sensors, payload capacity and perhaps stealth, the cheapness and endurance associated with UAVs quickly wither away, and the differences between manned and unmanned platforms become marginal at best.

However, in an age of increasingly constrained defence budgets, a 'belt and braces' approach becomes unaffordable, and there will inevitably be tension between funding UAVs and funding other systems which perform an overlapping mission.[58]   The US Congress has routinely voted more money for UAVs than the Pentagon requested, fearing that protectionist impulses were inhibiting innovation.[59]   In future, there is likely to be more and more direct competition between traditional programmes and UAV or UCAV contenders for the contracts and funding concerned. Aerial reconnaissance is already an area where unmanned systems have a very strong profile, placing manned reconnaissance platforms in significant jeopardy. New satellite programmes will also have to justify themselves against claims that persistent high altitude UAVs could do the same job at a less exorbitant cost.[60]   Armed UAVs have considerable potential to challenge future restocks or upgrades of cruise missiles, by offering a good chance of reusability while retaining a lack of human exposure.[61]   New manned bombers and even fighters will likewise face stiff competition from UCAV alternatives, and there may well be an attractive intermediate approach of a mix of manned and unmanned platforms working together in a single squadron. Since UAVs do not seem to offer unanswerable overall advantages across the full capability range, the inertia embodied in the current dominance of manned aircraft and satellites guarantees that any shift will be gradual at best, but it would be very surprising if the proportion of aerospace spending devoted to UAVs does not continue its upward trajectory as the century proceeds.[62]

Impact on US Aerospace Dominance   Just as Britain's industrial strength allowed it to retain naval primacy a century ago despite the obsolescence of its existing battlefleet in the face of the Dreadnought revolution, so it is the United States itself which is very much in the lead of the present proliferation of UAVs.[63]   In 2008, the US owned about 5,700 of the roughly 6,700 operational UAVs in the entire NATO alliance, including around 425 of the 520 or so HALE or MALE vehicles.[64]   As regards major peer competitors, China seems to place little emphasis on UAVs, despite fielding a number of different types. Russia's UAV programmes are now more prominent after a rather belated start, and they include the Tu-300 reconnaissance vehicle which is apparently capable of over 500 knots, and which may well form the basis of a future attack vehicle. However, since Russia and the United States both now spend only around 4% of their GDP on defence, Russia's efforts are inevitably constrained by the fact that its GDP is less than 15% of America's, even using favourable comparators such as 'Purchasing Power Parity'.[65]

There is a strong case that the increasing prominence of Uavs will actually *enhance* the aerospace dominance of the US, by playing to its strengths of high technology and network-centric warfare, and by finessing its residual casualty sensitivity (already much lower than it was a decade ago due to the twin blows of September 11th and the bloody wars in Iraq and Afghanistan). It is theoretically possible that a computer-savvy opponent could use the potential of unmanned systems to overcome its dearth of experienced aircrew and to surprise US forces with an overwhelming swarm of precisely targeted air vehicles.[66] It is also just about conceivable that a clever antagonist, through some combination of hacking, jamming and physical attack, could inflict catastrophic disruption on the entire networked infrastructure on which the US war effort (and especially its Uavs) depends. However, it seems more likely that the real challenge to US aerospace dominance will continue to lie in grinding and drawn out asymmetric resistance by elusive insurgents, always keen to damn the US for a misplaced strike or to inflict a spectacularly bloody attack of their own.

Impact on Service Specialisations Ballistic and cruise missiles, helicopters and satellites have all served to muddy the waters of the once fairly clear functional subdivision of military forces into soldiers, sailors and airmen. Uavs are no exception to this pattern, and by relocating aircrew from cockpits to remote video consoles on the other side of the world, while also providing soldiers with their own miniature hand-launched 'eye in the sky', they call even further into question the utility of a distinct category of air or aerospace power within the increasingly integrated and joint web which is modern military power as a whole. It was already the case that the proportion of actual flight crew within air forces was diminishing apace due to the concentration on fewer, more capable manned platforms, and, at the same time as British Army television adverts were (as I mentioned) highlighting the chance to control a tactical UAV, the Royal Air Force was championing its diverse ground branches under the recruiting slogan, 'You don't have to be a pilot to fly in the RAF'! This juxtaposition illustrates perfectly the blurring of traditional service roles in the new technological environment.

As one might expect, some aircrew have expressed serious reservations about the wisdom of a progressive shift from manned aircraft towards Uavs.[67] Encouragingly, however, most officers (including aircrew) seem to take a much more productive stance, avoiding inflammatory topics such as air force abolition, and focusing instead on the best and most effective way of employing Uavs within the overall joint force structure.[68] This contrasts significantly with British experience in the inter-war period, when battles over the independence of the newly-formed RAF spilled over into doctrine and inhibited inter-service cooperation, somewhat compromising British military effectiveness in the early years of World War Two.[69] There does still need to be clearer thinking about how to integrate UAV operation into service career tracks, and there are still some branches of service (especially navies) where the potential contribution of Uavs has perhaps not yet been taken fully on board, but overall, the depth and seriousness of the discussion of UAVs in Western defence literature (as referenced in this chapter) bodes well for a positive strategic impact from their increasing adoption in the years and decades to come.[70]

NOTES

[1] Directorate of Air Staff, *British Air Power Doctrine*, AP 3000, 3rd edition, (London: Ministry of Defence, 1999), p.1.2.1.

[2] *Ibid*, pp.1.2.3-9.

[3] Wayne Lee, *To Rise from Earth*, (London: Cassell, 2000), p.11.

[4] See Richard Hallion, 'Precision Air Attack in the Modern Era', in Richard Hallion (ed.), *Air Power Confronts an Unstable World*, (London: Brassey's, 1997).

[5] See Paul Mitchell, *Network Centric Warfare*, Adelphi Paper 385, (London: Routledge for IISS, 2006).

[6] On attempts to limit this vicious cycle, see Gerard Keijsper, *Joint Strike Fighter*, (Barnsley: Pen & Sword, 2007), ch.8.

[7] Annual US military spending on space exceeds $22bn, compared to only around $2bn for Western Europe as a whole (primarily France). See *Strategic Survey 2007*, (London: Routledge for IISS, 2007), pp.69-84.

[8] See Mark Wells, *Courage and Air Warfare*, (London: Frank Cass, 1995), C. Hyde, 'Casualty Aversion: Implications for Policy Makers and Senior Military Officers', *Aerospace Power Journal* 14/2, Summer 2000, and Mary Kelly, *"Good to Go"*, (Annapolis MA: Naval Institute Press, 1996).

[9] See Philip Sabin, 'Western Strategy in the New Era: The Apotheosis of Air Power?', in Andrew Dorman, Mike Smith & Matthew Uttley (eds.), *The Changing Face of Military Power* (London: Palgrave, 2001), 'US condemned as airstrike kills nine allies in another deadly blunder', *The Times*, October 23rd 2008, and 'US says sorry after wedding party is bombed in ambush', *The Times*, November 6th, 2008.

[10] See J Olsen (ed.), *Asymmetric Warfare* (Oslo: Royal Norwegian Air Force Academy, 2002).

[11] See Philip Sabin, 'The Counter-Air Contest', in Andrew Lambert & Arthur Williamson (eds.), *The Dynamics of Air Power*, (Bracknell: RAF Staff College, 1996).

[12] Rupert Smith, *The Utility of Force*, London: Allen Lane, 2005), and Harry Kemsley, 'Combat Air Power in Irregular Warfare', *RAF Air Power Review* 10/2, Summer 2007, pp.28-9.

[13] See Benjamin Lambeth, *NATO's Air War for Kosovo*, (Santa Monica CA: RAND, 2001), Neville Parton, 'Israel's 2006 Campaign in the Lebanon', *RAF Air Power Review* 10/2, Summer 2007, and Stephen Biddle & Jeffrey Friedman, *The 2006 Lebanon Campaign and the Future of Warfare*, (Carlisle PA: Strategic Studies Institute, 2008). On the general techniques which may be used to combat superior air power, see Philip Sabin, 'Air Strategy and the Underdog', in Peter Gray (ed.), *Air Power 21*, (London: The Stationery Office, 2000).

[14] *Unmanned Aircraft Systems Roadmap, 2005-2030*, (Washington DC: Office of the Secretary of Defense, 2005), pp.37-8

[15] *Strategic Survey 2007*, (London: Routledge for IISS, 2007), pp.74-5, and *The Military Balance 2008*, (London: Routledge for IISS, 2008), p.29.

[16] *Unmanned Aircraft Systems Roadmap, 2005-2030*, (Washington DC: Office of the Secretary of Defense, 2005), pp.56-7.

[17] Ibid, Appendices H & K, and John Drew *et al*, *Unmanned Air Vehicles End-to-End Support Considerations*, (Santa Monica CA: RAND, 2005).

[18] Andrea Nativi, 'Manned vs Unmanned', *JAPCC Journal* 3, 2006, and *The Military Balance 2008*, (London: Routledge for IISS, 2008), pp.455-60.

[19] See the *Unmanned Aircraft Systems Roadmap, 2005-2030*, (Washington DC: Office of the Secretary of Defense, 2005), pp.3-40.

[20] See James Hoffman & Charles Kamps, 'At the Crossroads: Future "Manning" for Unmanned Aerial Vehicles', *Air & Space Power Journal*, Spring 2005.

[21] See Hugh McDaid & David Oliver, *Robot Warriors*, (London: Orion, 1997), Laurence Newcome, *Unmanned Aviation*, (Barnsley: Pen & Sword, 2004), and Chip Thompson, 'F-16 UCAVs', *Aerospace Power Journal*, Spring 2000.

[22] *Unmanned Aircraft Systems Roadmap, 2005-2030*, (Washington DC: Office of the Secretary of Defense, 2005), pp.26 & 56.

[23] *The Joint Air Power Competence Centre Flight Plan for Unmanned Aircraft Systems in NATO*, (Cleve: JAPCC, March 2008), Annex B.

[24] *Unmanned Aircraft Systems Roadmap, 2005-2030*, (Washington DC: Office of the Secretary of Defense, 2005), pp.29-30, and Hugh McDaid & David Oliver, *Robot Warriors*, (London: Orion, 1997), pp.138-41.

[25] *Unmanned Aircraft Systems Roadmap, 2005-2030*, (Washington DC: Office of the Secretary of Defense, 2005), p.58.

[26] *Ibid*, pp.4 & 10, Jeffrey Ethell & Alfred Price, *Air War South Atlantic*, (London: Sidgwick & Jackson, 1983), ch.3, Benjamin Lambeth, *NATO's Air War for Kosovo*, (Santa Monica CA: RAND, 2001), pp.89-94, and 'Israeli drones destroy rocket-smuggling convoys in Sudan', *The Sunday Times*, March 29th 2009.

[27] *Unmanned Aircraft Systems Roadmap, 2005-2030*, (Washington DC: Office of the Secretary of Defense, 2005), pp.32-6, Dan Lewandowski, 'Exploiting a New High Ground', *JAPCC Journal* 3, 2006, Laurence Newcome, *Unmanned Aviation*, (Barnsley: Pen & Sword, 2004), ch.14, and *The Military Balance 2008*, (London: Routledge for IISS, 2008), p.458. On the technological challenges facing high altitude airships, see Kurt Hall, *Near Space*, Maxwell Paper 38, (Maxwell AL: Air University Press, 2006).

[28] On the blurring of the boundary between civilian and military surveillance, see 'Look Out and Up for New Spy in Sky', *The Times*, November 6th 2007, and 'Spy drone to patrol coast in hunt for people smugglers', *The Sunday Times*, December 2nd 2007.

[29] Benjamin Lambeth, *NATO's Air War for Kosovo*, (Santa Monica CA: RAND, 2001), pp.116-20.

[30] *Ibid*, pp.136-43 & 147-58.

[31] Hugh McDaid & David Oliver, *Robot Warriors*, (London: Orion, 1997), pp.32-47 & 68-9, Laurence Newcome, *Unmanned Aviation*, (Barnsley: Pen & Sword, 2004), ch.10, and 'Secrecy and denial as Pakistan lets US use airbase to hit its own militants', *The Times*, Feb.18th, 2009.

[32] *Ibid*, pp.61-5 & 94-7, and *Unmanned Aircraft Systems Roadmap, 2005-2030*, (Washington DC: Office of the Secretary of Defense, 2005), Appendix K.

[33] Williamson Murray & Robert Scales, *The Iraq War: A Military History*, (Cambridge MA: Harvard University Press, 2003), p.169.

[34] See Andy Evans, *Combat Search & Rescue*, (London: Arms & Armour, 1999), and Darrel Whitcomb, 'Rescue Operations in the Second Gulf War', *Air & Space Power Journal*, Spring 2005.

[35] See Kenneth Werrell, *Archie, Flak, AAA, and SAM*, Maxwell AL: Air University Press, 1988), pp.139-47, Lon Nordeen, *Air Warfare in the Missile Age*, 2nd edition, (Washington DC: Smithsonian Institution, 2002), pp.123-63, and Yair Dubester & Ido Pickel, '30 Years of Israeli UAV Experience', *JAPCC Journal* 3, 2006.

[36] Douglas Harpel, 'UAVs are Decisive Factor in Decline in Iraq IED Attacks', *Defence Systems Daily*, November 6th 2007, at **http://defence-data.com/current/page38536.htm**.

[37] On the continuing evolution of the air defence threat, even from lesser powers, see Benjamin Lambeth, *NATO's Air War for Kosovo*, (Santa Monica CA: RAND, 2001), pp.102-16, and Michael Knights, *Cradle of Conflict*, (Annapolis MD: Naval Institute Press, 2005), pp.230-5.

[38] 'Family of Marine killed by bomber demand better armour for troops', *The Glasgow Herald*, June 28th 2008.

[39] On the importance of surprise and seizing the initiative, see 'Secret convoy defies Taleban in epic bluff', *The Times*, September 3rd 2008.

[40] Interview with Wg Cdr Rich McMahon, DAS Ops UAV, Ministry of Defence, December 21st 2007. (CAOC stands for Combined Air Operations Centre.)

[41] Benjamin Lambeth, *NATO's Air War for Kosovo*, (Santa Monica CA: RAND, 2001), and Sarah Kreps, 'The 2006 Lebanon War: Lessons Learned', *Parameters*, Spring 2007.

[42] On the problems this poses for UAVs in dogfights, see Jeff Mustin, 'Future Employment of Unmanned Aerial Vehicles', *Aerospace Power Journal*, Summer 2002.

[43] *The Military Balance 2008*, (London: Routledge for IISS, 2008), p.459.

[44] Kurt Klausner, 'Will Bandwidth be the Major Limiting Factor of Future Air Operations?', *RAF Air Power Review* 6/2, Summer 2003.

[45] *Unmanned Aircraft Systems Roadmap, 2005-2030*, (Washington DC: Office of the Secretary of Defense, 2005), pp.47-51.

[46] *Ibid*, pp.70-1 & Appendix H, and Defence Science Board, *Unmanned Aerial Vehicles and Unmanned Combat Aerial Vehicles*, (Washington DC: Office of the Under Secretary of Defense for Acquisition, Technology and Logistics, February 2004), ch.3.

[47] *Unmanned Aircraft Systems Roadmap, 2005-2030*, (Washington DC: Office of the Secretary of Defense, 2005), Appendix F, and Mike Strong, 'Integrating UAV With Other Airspace Users', *JAPCC Journal* 3, 2006.

[48] *Unmanned Aircraft Systems Roadmap, 2005-2030*, (Washington DC: Office of the Secretary of Defense, 2005), Appendix K.

[49] *Ibid*, p.K-1, 'Georgian spy drones "shot down"', *The Times*, May 5th 2008, 'The "frozen conflict" that is thawing rapidly and could lead to a new war', *The Times*, May 20th 2008, and 'Predator Attrition', *Strategy Page*, December 20th 2007, at **http://www.strategypage.com/htmw/htairfo/articles/20071220.aspx**

[50] Philip Sabin, 'Air Strategy and the Underdog', in Peter Gray (ed.), *Air Power 21*, (London: The Stationery Office, 2000), Neville Parton, 'Israel's 2006 Campaign in the Lebanon', *RAF Air Power Review* 10/2, Summer 2007, and 'Gaza rockets put Israel's nuclear plant in battle zone', *The Times*, Jan. 2nd, 2009.

[51] *Strategic Survey 2007*, (London: Routledge for IISS, 2007), p.362, and 'Besieged rebels retaliate with air raid on capital', *The Times*, Feb. 21st, 2009.

[52] 'Iran uses UAV to Watch US Aircraft Carrier on Gulf Patrol', *Space War*, November 11th 2006, at **http://www.spacewar.com/reports/Iran_Uses_UAV_To_Watch_US_Aircraft_Carrier_On_Gulf_Patrol_999.html** , 'Terrorists Develop Unmanned Aerial Vehicles', *Center for Arms Control, Energy and Environmental Studies at MIPT*, December 6th, 2004, at **http://www.armscontrol.ru/UAV/mirsad1.htm** and 'Iranian UAVs over Israel', *Strategy Page*, August 9th 2006, at **http://www.strategypage.com/htmw/htairfo/articles/20060809.aspx**

[53] Hugh McDaid & David Oliver, *Robot Warriors*, (London: Orion, 1997), pp.32-47 & 68-9.

[54] John Stillion & David Orletsky, *Airbase Vulnerability to Conventional Cruise-Missile and Ballistic-Missile Attacks*, (Santa Monica CA: RAND, 1999), and Rex Kiziah, 'The Emerging Biocruise Threat', *Air & Space Power Journal*, Spring 2003.

[55] For a critical perspective, see Lawrence Freedman, *The Revolution in Strategic Affairs*, Adelphi Paper 318, (New York: Oxford University Press for IISS, 1998).

[56] 'Changing face of war: now a pilot in Las Vegas can blast a sniper in a Baghdad apartment', *The Times*, March 14th 2008.

[57] Tom Hobbins, 'Unmanned Aircraft Systems: Refocusing the Integration of Air & Space Power', *JAPCC Journal* 3, 2006. For a similar view from a non-military and non-Western observer, see Manjeet Pardesi, 'Unmanned Aerial Vehicles/ Unmanned Combat Aerial Vehicles: Likely Missions and Challenges for the Policy-Relevant Future', *Air & Space Power Journal*, Fall 2005.

[58] There may also, of course, be overlaps between UAV missions themselves – see David Hume, *Integration of Weaponized Unmanned Aircraft into the Air-to-Ground System*, Maxwell Paper 41, (Maxwell AL: Air University Press, 2007).

[59] US General Accounting Office, *Force Structure: Improved Strategic Planning Can Enhance DoD's Unmanned Aerial Vehicles Efforts*, Report to the Chairman, Subcommittee on Tactical Air and Land Forces, Committee on Armed Services, House of Representatives, GAO-04-342, (Washington DC: GAO, March 2004).

[60] Mark Steves, 'Near Space 2015', *Air & Space Power Journal*, Summer 2006.

[61] Robert Chapman, 'Unmanned Combat Aerial Vehicles: Dawn of a New Age?', *Aerospace Power Journal*, Summer 2002.

[62] On likely ways ahead in the near term, see *The Joint Air Power Competence Centre Flight Plan for Unmanned Aircraft Systems in NATO*, (Cleve: JAPCC, March 2008).

[63] Robert Massie, *Dreadnought*, (New York: Random House, 1991).

[64] *The Joint Air Power Competence Centre Flight Plan for Unmanned Aircraft Systems in NATO*, (Cleve: JAPCC, March 2008), Annex B.

[65] Hugh McDaid & David Oliver, *Robot Warriors*, (London: Orion, 1997), pp.63-9, Phillip Saunders & Erik Quam, 'China's Air Force Modernization', *Joint Force Quarterly* 47, 2007, *The Military Balance 2008*, (London: Routledge for IISS,

2008), pp.18-29, 205-25 & 376-81, and Eugene Kogan, 'Russian UAVs making a comeback', at **http://www.isn.ethz.ch/news/sw/details.cfm?id=15032**

[66] See Francois Heisbourg, *The Future of Warfare*, Predictions 2, (London: Phoenix, 1997), pp.26-9.

[67] Jeff Mustin, 'Flesh and Blood: The Call for the Pilot in the Cockpit', *Air & Space Power Journal*, Chronicles Online, 2001, at **http://www.airpower.maxwell.af.mil/ airchronicles/cc/mustin.html**

[68] James Fitzsimonds & Thomas Mahnken, 'Military Officer Attitudes Toward UAV Adoption: Exploring Institutional Impediments to Innovation', *Joint Force Quarterly* 46, 2007. A good example of this constructive approach is David Deptula, 'Unmanned Aircraft Systems: Taking Strategy to Task', and 'Air and Space Power Going Forward', both in *Joint Force Quarterly* 49, 2008.

[69] Brian Bond & Williamson Murray, 'The British Armed Forces, 1918-39', in Allan Millett & Williamson Murray (eds.), *Military Effectiveness*, vol.II, (Boston: Allen & Unwin, 1988).

[70] For a more detailed and focused treatment of specifically British aspects of unmanned air systems, see the House of Commons Defence Committee's 13th report of Session 2007-08, *The contribution of Unmanned Aerial Vehicles to ISTAR Capability*, (London: The Stationery Office, HC 535, August 2008).

UNMANNED AERIAL VEHICLES – PROGRESS
AND CHALLENGE

AVM Prof R A Mason

Prologue

On February 25th 2009 a USAF fighter shot down an unmanned Iranian surveillance drone over Iraq, 60 miles north east of Baghdad.[1] The incident, which provoked no reaction from Iran, was not reported until March 16th. Six days later the British Press described the RAF's No 39 Squadron carrying out its historical reconnaissance role. Now however, its aircraft were unmanned MQ-9 Reapers, controlled and "flown" from Creech Air Force Base in Arizona, turned round on an airfield in Afghanistan, and delivering precision munitions as well as reconnaissance.[2] In April 2009 the US Marine Corps was reported to be seeking an unmanned cargo aircraft for resupply of forward operating bases.[3]

Assumptions amid Uncertainty

As explained in earlier chapters in this volume, UAVs already discharge many roles, from short range reconnaissance to long endurance surveillance and weapon delivery. They are operated by air forces, armies, and navies. How far they will replace manned aircraft remains uncertain. In its second century, air power must be prepared to contribute to policy and strategy across a very wide potential spectrum of conflict, from insurgency to inter-state conflict. Amid the uncertainty, factors may be confidently identified which will influence UK decisions about the procurement and employment of UAVs and associated systems. Some will encourage their speedy development, others may be more problematical.

Resource Constraints

Resources allocated to defence are likely to reduce in real terms. Inevitably, procurement and life cycle cost comparisons will heavily influence every debate about investment in UAVs. As they incorporate more and more on-board systems and probably stealth technology, the gap between their procurement costs and those of comparable manned aircraft will decrease, as Philip Sabin has explained. Life cycle costs will however offer savings. For example, the endurance or combat radius of a UAV, like the manned aircraft, is influenced by weight, payload and fuel capacity. UAV fuel consumption will be substantially less than that of its manned equivalent. Predator B can fly for 17 hours, much of them on auto pilot, and until a UAV becomes completely autonomous, it will probably require four or six crews in sequence to control it remotely. In comparison, the B-2 Spirit can reach much further, but to do so requires not just a two man crew but all the personnel, aircraft, infra-structure and resources associated with in-flight refuelling.

The comparative ground support costs are also likely to favour the UAV, even though ground crew numbers are difficult to compare when the maintenance costs of even the most complex aircraft systems may be reduced by replacement items, computerised fault identification and repair and multi-skilled personnel. Moreover, UAV "ground crew" include the remote controllers, usually pilot and systems operator. In No 39 Squadron in early 2009, a Reaper crew comprised a combat experienced, commissioned pilot and a senior NCO weapon systems operator. In the same period the United States Air Force began a trial to train non-rated personnel as UAV controllers. The question of how far qualified aircrew are needed to control UAVs has more than just financial implications, which will be addressed below. Personnel costs are however a major budgetary factor and undoubted savings would accrue from a reduction in the numbers of trained pilots.

Overall, the substitution of UAVs for manned aircraft in similar roles is likely to offer significant resource savings. Such savings are particularly attractive to governments under acute pressure to reduce defence expenditure. Other UAV advantages will increase that attraction.

Casualty sensitivity

Between the end of the Cold War and the Iraq conflict which began in 2003, very few casualties were sustained by the UK armed forces and allies. Casualty sensitivity has become and will remain a permanent feature of conflict. But, after 9/11 the US was prepared to accept a much higher level of casualties in Afghanistan and Iraq than in the previous conflict over Kosovo.

In referring to that conflict, General Wesley Clarke wrote:

"But we had to move the campaign along some general paths, in addition to minding the legal constraints in the order. I termed these 'measures of merit'... I dropped them onto the command: 'As we start working through this, there are three measures of merit for the operation overall from the military standpoint. The first measure of merit is not to lose aircraft, 'minimize the loss of aircraft.' This addressed Mike Short's biggest concern - to prevent the loss of aircrews. It drove our decisions on tactics, targets, and which air planes could participate.[4]

To much of the US general public, the Kosovo campaign seemed to be peripheral to its national interests. Casualty tolerance was low. Conversely, after September 2001, the "war on terrorism" was driven by core perceptions of national security, and public acceptance of military casualties expanded proportionately. To a certain extent UK casualty sensitivity in all operations will also reflect the issues at stake, and influence the evaluation of the UAV.

There is however a more persistent consideration about casualties. General Clarke went on to observe:

'But I was motivated by a larger political-military rationale. If we wanted to keep this campaign going indefinitely, we had to protect our air fleet. Nothing would hurt us more with public opinion than headlines that screamed, 'NATO LOSES TEN AIRPLANES IN TWO DAYS'. Take losses like that, divide it into the total number of aircraft committed, and the time limits on the campaign would be clear. Milosovic could wait us out."[5]

The General coupled public perception with the potential operational impact of losses in a limited conflict. As the armed forces have been reduced in numbers, the operational value of the remainder has increased. The RAF no longer has a large pool of trained aircrew on ground duties available for rapid operational refreshing and reinforcement of the front line. Nor does a greatly reduced training structure have the potential for rapid expansion, as it did in Trenchard's day. It is not so much the loss of aircraft, but of highly and expensively trained aircrew. Whatever the issues at stake, the ability of the UAV to reduce aircrew vulnerability will remain a hard nosed resource attraction, quite apart from its obvious impact on aircrew morale.

Diplomatic Advantage

UAVs not only obviate the risk of aircrew casualties, they have a much lower political profile. By the nature of their activities, surveillance and reconnaissance flights usually go unreported. But the shooting down of Gary Power's U-2 near Sverdlovsk in 1960 had an immediate and dramatic impact on US-USSR relations. Several other Cold War incidents of intercepted over-flights of sovereign air space prompted diplomatic confrontation. The loss or internment of aircrew heightened public concern, publicised failure and embarrassed the parent Service. The remains of Gary Powers' aircraft were for many years a popular exhibit in the Soviet Air Museum in Moscow. The interception of a single "Stealth" USAF F-117 in 1999 made international headlines and gave President Milosovic a rare military and media coup. In contrast, the remains in the Serbian Air Museum in Belgrade of a USAF Predator, also shot down in 1999, are an unremarked curiosity. In early 2009, in a period of acute US-Iranian tension, the shooting down of the Iranian reconnaissance UAV well inside Iraqi air space passed without comment by both US and Iran governments and was largely unreported by the media when it was finally disclosed.

Vulnerability

While the Iranian Ababil 3 was shot down over Iraq, British and other allied UAVs were operating with comparative impunity over Afghanistan, where there was no opposition in the air, and no coordinated air defences below them. At the moment, UAVs are defenceless: slow moving, scarcely manoeuvrable and probably announcing their presence by electronic communication or sensors. As their size has increased, so has their visibility. The Predator C is more than 43 feet long with a wing span of 66 feet. The Harrier GR9 is 47 feet long with a wing span of 30 feet. The incorporation of stealth technology will reduce combat vulnerability to a certain extent, but control of the air will remain an essential prerequisite for UAV operations at any level of conflict. For the foreseeable future, that control will depend in the air on manned aircraft capable of establishing it. Aircraft such as Typhoon 2 will remain indispensable to all operations in the air, on the ground and at sea.

It is difficult to avoid the conclusion that just as the massive contribution of the manned reconnaissance aircraft in World War One swiftly stimulated measures to destroy them, in this century UAVs will face a similar response. While stealth configuration will reduce their vulnerability to detection and attack from the air or ground, as Philip Sabin observed, their communications will be vulnerable to interference, however stealthy their configuration. Any system which depends on electronic control is vulnerable to electronic disruption. The acquisition by irregular forces of localised jammers for example, is inevitable. UAVs will become involved in electronic warfare recalling that waged by manned aircraft and their opposition in World War 2. Autonomous operation would reduce hostile opportunities for interference but deny opportunities for over-riding human recovery.

Even in a benign environment, UAVs are reported to have suffered a "significant" accident rate. By April 2009, of 195 Predators purchased by the Pentagon, 55 had been lost in "Class A mishaps" which by inference excluded any casualties to hostile action. The overall loss rate was 10 accidents per 100,000 flying hours for Predator and 12.7 for Reaper, with one third of the losses attributed to pilot error, others to hardware failure and landing problems.[6] The UK lost 71 UAVs in Iraq between 2003 and 2007[7] and a further 27 in Afghanistan by February 2009[8] . These losses were incurred in the comparatively early years of UAV but dependence on remote control inevitably reduces opportunities and time for reaction to an emergency or miscalculation. Autonomous take offs and landing would help and stealth technology could reduce combat losses, but not necessarily accidents rates. Even if a UAV cost one third of a manned aircraft performing similar roles, losses at several times the rate of the manned alternative could quickly erode any cost benefit.

The hub of the UAV system is the ground control centre (GCC). In early 2009 the RAF No 39 squadron's GCC in Arizona was several thousand miles away from its combat theatre in Afghanistan. In World War One, Trenchard famously sought to win air superiority by seeking out German aircraft on their own airfields: the origins of the counter-air role. If the UK and its allies continue to retain command of the air, that option will not be available to an enemy, either against UAV forward operating bases or GCCs. It may be assumed that operating bases in theatre will benefit from the airfield protection given in Afghanistan by the RAF Regiment and other ground defences. Duplication and mobility will reduce the vulnerability of GCCs, but to an opponent, Creech AFB is a military target, however far away from the combat theatre. Just as the western domination by manned aircraft of recent conflicts has stimulated hostile asymmetric responses, so the increasing importance of the UAV will stimulate countermeasures which will seek to render command of the air irrelevant. GCCs will be threatened by kinetic, cyber and even hostile media attack.

War fighter or remote controller?

In a previous chapter on the UAV in the context of the Laws of Armed Conflict (LOAC), Alison Mardell largely concentrated on the legal responsibilities of the authorising and controlling decision makers. She demonstrated conclusively that UAV operations must conform to the LOAC even when the UAV, such as Taranis, was operating autonomously. She also explained the ambivalent legal position of civilian controllers or support services. The contemporary problem of LOAC interpretation is that they were conceived in an age and for circumstances when the distinction between combatants and civilians was comparatively straightforward. Even then, protagonists of strategic bombing held that arms industry and oil refineries, together with their civilian work forces, were legitimate targets. Now, the combatant targets of the UAV are often indistinguishable from their civilian neighbours while the opposition makes no distinction between combatants and civilians in its own war fighting.

The UAV controller may be well away from combat. There are sound military and morale reasons for enhancing the capability of the war fighter by removing him/her from immediate danger. Whatever the view of the international lawyers, there will be little military doubt that the UAV controller is a combatant. A "civilian" UAV controller becomes a contradiction in terms, even when clothed with the ambiguity of the CIA. The most recent precedent is the ballistic missile controller in the silo beneath the Nebraska hills or Russian steppes. The UAV controller is a war fighter; a definition which will present more difficulties to parent Services than to international lawyers.

In the Royal Air Force, as Seb Cox explained in his Chapter, there has always been a shadow hierarchy within the official hierarchical structure. Only a very small proportion of the Service has ever been involved in combat even though ground crew frequently suffered casualties from enemy air attack, and from the later stages of the Cold War onwards have carried arms and been trained to withstand attacks on airfields and other installations. In recent years, navigators have shared many of the responsibilities of high command, until in 2009 Air Marshal Sir Stuart Peach became Chief of UK Operations, but RAF Commanders-in-Chief and Chiefs of the Air Staff have been drawn almost exclusively from fighter or bomber pilots.

Operationally however, the distinction between "combat" aircraft and others has become increasingly blurred. In the whole of the Balkan Wars the only western aircrew to be shot down and killed were flying an Italian Air Force G-222 transport. Numerous decorations for valour in Iraq and Afghanistan have reflected helicopter and fixed wing transport operations in hostile environments, perhaps best epitomised by the award of a Distinguished Flying Cross, for valour in the face of the enemy, to helicopter pilot Flight Lieutenant

Michelle Goodman in 2008. It is highly likely that the broadening of combat experience across different roles will sooner or later be reflected in the high command of the RAF, as it is already in the USAF and other air forces. If, as may be confidently assumed, the UCAV makes an increasing contribution to UK air power, where will "war fighting" UCAV controllers fit in the future hierarchy?

Will controllers continue to be pilots on ground tours? Perhaps the fundamental question should be: "How best can the RAF develop the expertise, judgement and command experience essential for the most operationally cost effective integration of the UCAV with manned aircraft?" Alternating front line squadron appointments with UCAV control would enhance expertise in joint UCAV-manned aircraft operations but would raise questions about training costs and even about sustained flight pay. Employing aircrew other than pilots would draw upon operational awareness but would require additional pilot training. Employing ground crew would create the most complex career management problems unless a new specialist Trade or Branch was established, which in turn would complicate subsequent fusion of operational experience at high command level.

Those considerations apply equally to UAV reconnaissance/ surveillance and air to surface attack operations. If however the UCAV comes to operate in the air-to-air role, the argument for a trained combat pilot controller becomes much stronger. Such practical issues may in the longer term be more important than the more philosophical question of who is a warrior and who isn't.

Roles

Wing Commander McMahon imaginatively and comprehensively explores the possibilities of UAV operations. Their basic attributes have been amply discussed in previous chapters. In the near future their primary contribution will be to reconnaissance and surveillance. Air power has moved on, from an age when locating a target was relatively straightforward but hitting it precisely was not, to environments where precision strike is almost taken for granted but locating and confirming a target can be much more difficult. The demand in all theatres for ISTAR will continue to exceed supply. As with early warning of hostile activity in the last century, anomaly detection, whether in human activity or in the appearance of roads and culverts, will remain essential in counter insurgency, but not so easy to acquire. Now, as then, intelligence from human sources will be a valuable component. Operational awareness must lead to understanding. Extended surveillance, preferably covert, over lengthy periods, short range reconnaissance and battle damage assessment will be essential for all operations. In the air it can best be achieved by medium or high level long endurance UAS such as Predator, Reaper or Global Hawk or repeated shorter range sorties by Watch Keeper, Desert Hawk, Herti and their successors, procured within an integrated UAV programme.

The extent of UCAV development is more debatable but it will increasingly share the combat roles hitherto the exclusive domain of the manned aircraft.

The offensive potential of a UCAV which could loiter for many hours without detection, identify a target and strike precisely and swiftly is obvious. So much so that the decision in 2009 by US Defense Secretary Robert Gates to include armed Uavs within the USAF fighter (ie fighter/bomber) structure, prompted fears in the USAF that "Reapers and later Predator Cs, would substitute for F-35 JSFs".[9] The UK Minister of Defence for Equipment and Support Quinton Davies indicated in April 2009 that UCAV would figure prominently in future equipment programmes.[10] RAF considerations for a future deep strike capability inevitably include UCAV, equipped with kinetic and non-kinetic weapons.

In the UK however, a force mix of UCAV and manned aircraft may not be so easy to achieve because the procurement decision would not rest with the RAF alone. In the face of constrained and probably reduced Defence expenditure, expansion of the contemporary manned combat aircraft front line by the addition of UCAVs is inconceivable. If the CAS or Commander in Chief of Air Command of the day sought to reduce the number of manned aircraft in order to release funds for UCAV purchase, there is no guarantee that such funds would be allocated in that way. Not only would the Treasury be looking for benefits but the UCAV proposals would have to compete with programmes in the other services. If however the RAF is to derive the greatest operational advantage from the integration UCAV into the front line, such a guarantee, however frail, is essential.

The UCAV can be expected to play an increased role in defence suppression. Christina Goulter notes the use of Israeli UAVs in 1982 to trigger Syrian Air defences before their destruction by manned aircraft. In future, UCAVs will attack air defences by themselves, a role which would be considerably enhanced by stealth configuration. There are likely to be progressive stages in the development of UCAVs for air-to-air combat. The first might be the installation of infra-red or early warning radar self defence systems which would autonomously react to threats, while the UCAV otherwise remained under remote control. That stage would entail resolving a relatively straightforward weight, payload, and risk cost/benefit equation. The second stage might be the incorporation of air-to-air weapons which, coupled with on-board sensors, would allow the controller to engage identified targets. That would require a further, more complex technological solution but still within the envelope of remote control. The third stage, almost certainly more than a generation away, would be the delegation of defensive systems to an autonomous UCAV which would discharge all the aggressive tasks of the air superiority manned fighter. Alison Mardell examines the sensitive legal issues surrounding autonomy, which would need to be added to the formidable technological advances required to replicate the contribution of the aircrew in a manned air superiority aircraft.

It is difficult to envisage RAF introduction of unmanned transport aircraft, although the USMC initiative is likely to be carefully scrutinised. Presumably the Marine Corps is considering the potential reduction in air crew exposure in short range supply sorties in a hostile environment. UAV savings in endurance and payload are unlikely to be significant in simply omitting aircrew from transport aircraft. The RAF may be expected to concentrate on ISTAR UAV and multi-role UCAV.

Conclusion

Air power is about the military exploitation of air and space by man, not necessarily with man. The UAV is already evolving into the multi-role UCAV, reflecting trends in manned combat aircraft. The advantages of lower costs, reduced casualty risk, long endurance and low political profile, will encourage UAV increasingly to replace, not just complement, the manned aircraft in many traditional roles. Technology and experience may be expected to increase capabilities and reduce attrition rates. Problems of air space integration and international legality are likely to be soluble. Autonomous operation is more likely to be constrained by the need for human presence in the control system in conflicts where complex situational awareness and reaction to the unexpected are likely to be required. It is not the technology of the UCAV which presents the challenge, but its intellectual mastery. The RAF must devise a structure which will develop the expertise, judgement and command experience essential for the most effective operational integration of the UCAV with manned aircraft.

NOTES

[1] The Guardian Tuesday 17th March 2009.
[2] The Sunday Telegraph 22nd March 2009.
[3] Aviation Week and Space Technology, 13th April 2009.[4] General Wesley K Clarke, "Waging Modern War", Public Affairs New York 2001, pp 182-3.
[5] ibid.
[6] Aviation Week and Space Technology, May 4th 2009.
[7] Flight International, June 6th 2007.
[8] Statement to House of Commons by Secretary of State for Defence, 27th February 2009.
[9] Aviation Week and Space Technology, April 20th 2009.
[10] Addressing a Royal Aeronautical Society Conference, London, "Aerospace 2009", 21st April 2009.

NOTES

NOTES

NOTES

NOTES

NOTES